MOTOR RACING
AND
RECORD BREAKING

Frontispiece

1. THE DERBY-MILLER BREAKING RECORDS AT LINAS-MONTLHÈRY

From a drawing by F. Gordon Crosby. By kind permission of the "Autocar."

MOTOR RACING
AND
RECORD BREAKING

By
G. E. T. EYSTON
and
BARRÉ LYNDON

This edition digitally re-mastered and
published by JM Classic Editions © 2007
Original text © GET Eyston & B Lyndon 1935

ISBN 978-1-905217-89-2

All rights reserved. No part of this book subject
to copyright may be reproduced in any form or
by any means without prior permission in writing
from the publisher.

G. E. T. EYSTON

An Appreciation by S. C. H. DAVIS

GEORGE EYSTON first achieved success just after the War, when he became prominent at Brooklands track driving an Aston-Martin; from that he went on to drive Bugattis, including a very famous 2,300 c.c. machine, which was one of the fastest of its type, and a super-charged, straight-eight, 1½-litre which ran in the British Grand Prix and at Boulogne in 1927. But what really made his name was record-breaking, for George was one of the first people to tackle this as a very serious job, and it is rare that a year goes by without his achieving something quite exciting, either at the Montlhèry track in France or elsewhere.

The number of cars which he has driven or prepared for records must be legion; no other driver has had more different types and makes on the track for records, and quite often it seemed to his friends that no sooner had he broken one set of records with one car than he started off on another series with another car, while in the background he was busy with the preparation of a third machine. It is impossible to go into a full list of George's achievements, but the outstanding drives were 100 miles in the hour with a 750 c.c. M.G., 120 miles in the hour with the same machine, the world's hour record with the big Panhard, and the long-distance records with Riley, Hotchkiss, and Singer. All this time he was also driving in road and track races of every kind and type, so that no race was really complete without him. And then finally came his very magnificent effort away over in America with the gigantic Rolls-Royce-engined car, when he not only recaptured the world's hour record, but took the world's twenty-four-hour record into the bargain.

George, as a matter of fact, differs from most other drivers. He is, for example, far more interested in the technical side of his cars than the majority of drivers are to-day, and a great proportion of his success is due to this fact. He is usually extremely solemn, but can show all the verve and excitement that anybody could wish, and no man has stood the usual cheery leg-pulling with greater equanimity, one of the subjects for jest usually being the club-armchair type of driving seat which George prefers above all others.

His running commentary on the situation while his car is at the pits being refilled is always a considerable delight, but there isn't a man in existence who is less affected by exciting occurrences, and not only did he get out of hospital after the M.G. caught fire during records quicker than the medical profession desired, but limping about immediately he proceeded to prepare yet another car for more records. Further, he simply will not admit defeat. He attempted one day to restart the engine of a racing car by pushing it single-handed and then jumping in. It was a very difficult task, as can well be imagined, and George had at least six attempts during which the unbelievers rejoiced, but on the seventh he actually did get the engines started and drove away in triumph; and there is no doubt in my mind that he would have gone on all that day and most of the next until he actually did succeed.

CONTENTS

	PAGE
G. E. T. EYSTON	v
A BIOGRAPHICAL NOTE BY S. C. H. DAVIS	
NOTE OF ACKNOWLEDGMENT	viii
LIST OF ILLUSTRATIONS	ix

CHAPTER
I. EARLY YEARS	1
II. ROAD RACING	10
III. TRACK RACING	24
IV. ROUND-THE-HOUSES RACES	38
V. PIT-WORK	46
VI. RECORD BREAKING	54
VII. HILL CLIMBING	62
VIII. RACING IN AMERICA	69
IX. ENDURANCE RACING	77
X. RACING RISKS	88
XI. PERSONALITIES	98

LIST OF ILLUSTRATIONS

NO.	TITLE	SOURCE
1	(*Frontispiece*) The Derby-Miller breaking records at Linas-Montlhèry	*From a drawing by F. Gordon Crosby*
2	Otto von Morgen	*H. von Perkhammer*
3	Restarting after a Pit-stop	*H. von Perkhammer*
4	Lautenschlager on a Mercédès in 1914	*The Autocar*
5	The Grand Prix de Monaco at Monte Carlo	*Wide World*
6	Cars being examined at Brescia	*Fumagalli*
7	The Tripoli Grand Prix	*Vitt. Genah*
8	Racing over Sand at Skegness	*Sport and General*
9	Racing over Ice in Sweden	*Central Press*
10	Rudolf Caracciola on the Monza Track	*Fumagalli*
11	The Napier-Railton at Montlhèry	*Wide World*
12	Caracciola's Mercédès in the 1934 Coppa Acerbo	*Fumagalli*
13	Opening of the Grand Prix de la Marne	*Wide World*
14	Three Alfa-Romeos in the Grand Prix de la Marne	*Wide World*
15	Caracciola's Mercédès at Tripoli, 1935	*Fumagalli*
16	Spectators at the Grand Prix de Tunisie	*Wide World*
17	The Start of the French Grand Prix	*Central Press*
18	Conditions in the Grand Prix of Algiers	*Wide World*
19	Hans von Stuck in the 1934 French Grand Prix	*Motor Sport*
20	An M.G. Car in Newtownards Square	*Central Press*
21	Racing at Donington Park	*Motor Sport*
22	'Charley' Dodson winning the 1934 T.T. Race	*Central Press*
23	The Start of the Grand Prix of Czechoslovakia	*Wide World*
24	The Penya Rhin Grand Prix, Barcelona	*Wide World*
25	On the Lasarte Circuit, Spanish Grand Prix	*Wide World*
26	Light and Shadow at Brooklands	*Wide World*
27	A Car push-started by Mechanics	*H. von Perkhammer*
28	A Start on the Avus Track, Berlin	*Presse-Photo, Berlin*

LIST OF ILLUSTRATIONS—continued

NO.	TITLE	SOURCE
29	A Bugatti in the rain at Brooklands	*Wide World*
30	Aerial View of Indianapolis Speedway	*Wide World*
31	Start of the Indianapolis 500 miles Race	*Planet News*
32	At Culver City Speedway	*Keystone*
33	The Start of a Race at Avus	*Planet News*
34	Two Auto-Unions at Monza	*Fumagalli*
35	Five Cars bunched in a Turn at Monza	*Fumagalli*
36	At the Nurburg Ring, Germany	*Planet News*
37	The Grand Prix of Pau	*Wide World*
38	Luigi Fagioli at Monte Carlo	*Fumagalli*
39	On the Monaco Circuit, 1935	*Sport and General*
40	Racing along the Promenade at Nice	*Central Press*
41	'Freddie' Dixon in the Mannin Beg Race	*The Autocar*
42	Count Trossi in the Grand Prix de Vichy	*Wide World*
43	In the First Circuito di Biella, 1934	*Fumagalli*
44	Achille Varzi in the Biella Race	*Fumagalli*
45	The Finish of the Mannin Moar, 1935	*The Autocar*
46	Whitney Straight's Maserati at Montreux	*Wide World*
47	The Opel Rocket Car	*Sport and General*
48	A French Car designed for World's Records	*Wide World*
49	An Auto-Union at the Pits	*H. von Perkhammer*
50	Preparations before the Start	*H. von Perkhammer*
51	Pit Signals	From 'Der Kraftfahrsport' (*Verkehrsverlag, Berlin*)
52	A Pit-stop during the Bol d'Or Race	*Wide World*
53	An Auto-Union at the Pits	From 'Der Kraftfahrsport' (*Verkehrsverlag, Berlin*)
54	At the Pits on the Monza Track	*Wide World*
55	Concentrated Pit-work on Varzi's Car	*Fumagalli*
56	Dixon's Car at the Pits in the 500 miles Race, 1934	*Motor Sport*
57	Whitney Straight with a Duesenberg at Brooklands	*Keystone*
58	The 'Magic Midget' at Pendine	*Topical Press*
59	Hans von Stuck on the Avus Track, 1934	*Keystone*
60	A Diesel-engined Car at Linas-Montlhéry	*Agence Rol, Paris*
61	An Adler Saloon attacking Records at Avus	*Planet News*
62	Replenishment and Wheel-changing at Montlhéry	*Wide World*
63	Sir Malcolm Campbell at Daytona	*Sport and General*
64	'Blue Bird' being made ready at Daytona	*Sport and General*
65	Sir Malcolm Campbell's 'Blue Bird'	*Sport and General*

LIST OF ILLUSTRATIONS—*continued*

NO.	TITLE	SOURCE
66	Caracciola on the Avus Track, Berlin	*Wide World*
67	The 'Silver Bullet'	*Central Press*
68	Hans Villiez von Stuck	*Central Press*
69	A specially streamlined Auto-Union	*Fumagalli*
70	A frontal View of the same Car	*Fumagalli*
71	The *Bimotore* Alfa-Romeo	*Wide World*
72	Bonneville Salt-beds, Utah	*G. E. T. Eyston*
73	Capt. G. E. T. Eyston's Car, 'Speed of the Wind'	*Barratt's*
74	The Hill Climb up the Stelvio Pass	*Sport and General*
75	An E.R.A. at Shelsley Walsh, 1935	*W. J. Brunell*
76	Whitney Straight at Mont Ventoux	*Wide World*
77	In the Mulders' Hill Climb, South Africa	*Topical Press*
78	On the Mont Ventoux Hill Climb	*Wide World*
79	Altoona Speedway, Pennsylvania	*Wide World*
80	An American Dirt Track Event	*Planet News*
81	The Langhorne Dirt Track, Pennsylvania	*Wide World*
82	The Midget Car Championship, California	*Wide World*
83	Midget Cars at Los Angeles	*Wide World*
84	Start of the Grand Prix d'Endurance, Le Mans	*Wide World*
85	The winning Lagonda at Le Mans, 1935	*Wide World*
86	The winning Alfa-Romeo at Le Mans, 1934	*Wide World*
87	During the night at Le Mans	*Fox Photos*
88	Start of a Brooklands 'Double-Twelve' Race	*Fox Photos*
89	During the Targa Abruzzo	*Fumagalli*
90	The winning Bentley, 'Double-Twelve' Race, 1930	*Fox Photos*
91	The Start of the Bol d'Or, near Paris	*Wide World*
92	An M.G. Magnette in the Mille Miglia, Italy	*Romolo del Papa*
93	The Winners of the Mille Miglia, 1935	*Fumagalli*
94	A Crash at Le Mans	*Wide World*
95	A Crash on a California Dirt Track	*Wide World*
96	A Crash on the Woodbridge Dirt Track, New Jersey	*Wide World*
97	A Crash in the Tourist Trophy Race, 1934	*Central Press*
98	A Crash at Legion Ascot Speedway	*Planet News*
99	After a Series of Smashes at Monza	*Fumagalli*
100	The Wreckage of Guy Moll's Machine	*Fumagalli*
101	Extinguishing a Car at Brooklands, 1933	*Fox Photos*

LIST OF ILLUSTRATIONS—*continued*

NO.	TITLE	SOURCE
102	A Crash at Indianapolis	*Wide World*
103	Nurses in a First-aid Station at Avus	*H. von Perkhammer*
104	The Loss of a Front Wheel at Woodbridge	*Wide World*
105	After a Crash in Barcelona	*Wide World*
106	A Collision on an American Dirt Track	*Wide World*
107	A Somersault at Los Angeles	*Wide World*
108	A Crash on the North Curve, Indianapolis	*Planet News*
109	Result of a Skid at Brooklands, 1934	*Sport and General*
110	The late Sir Henry Segrave	*The Autocar*
111	Sir Malcolm Campbell	*H. von Perkhammer*
112	Louis Chiron	*Wide World*
113	Tazio Nuvolari	*Wide World*
114	Rudolf Caracciola	*H. von Perkhammer*
115	Achille Varzi	*Fumagalli*
116	Hans Villiez von Stuck	*Fumagalli*
117	The late Guy Moll	*H. von Perkhammer*
118	Luigi Fagioli	*Fumagalli*
119	Whitney Straight	*The Autocar*
120	Barney Oldfield	*Planet News*
121	Mrs. Gwenda Stewart	*Wide World*
122	The late J. G. Parry Thomas	*The Autocar*
123	Tommy Milton	*Planet News*
124	Lord Howe	*H. von Perkhammer*
125	John Cobb	*Wide World*
126	'Wild Bill' Cummings	*Wide World*
127	Kelly Petillo	*Wide World*
128	Hon. Brian Lewis	*The Autocar*
129	'Tim' Rose-Richards	*The Autocar*
130	The late Sir Henry Birkin	*Keystone*
131	F. W. ('Freddie') Dixon	*Associated Press*
132	Captain G. E. T. Eyston with Albert Denly	*Sport and General*

2 OTTO VON MORGEN, THE GERMAN DRIVER, REGISTERS DISAPPOINTMENT AFTER HIS CAR HAS FALLEN OUT OF A RACE

3 RESTARTING AFTER A PIT-STOP. THE CAR IS AN AUTO-UNION

CHAPTER I
EARLY YEARS

ANY survey of the conditions which have governed the evolution of motor racing in the past must necessarily be brief, because the world's first motor race was held only forty years ago. It started from the Place d'Armes, Versailles, at noon on June 11th, 1895, and the course was to Bordeaux and back, a distance of seven hundred and thirty-two miles.

The event was won by Emile Levassor on a 4 h.p. Panhard, at an average speed of 14·9 m.p.h. He covered the distance in 48 hours 47 minutes, and drove entirely without relief. Incidentally, a year earlier, a rally known as the *Course des Voitures sans Chevaux* had been organized, involving a run from Paris to Rouen, but it is generally conceded that the Paris-Bordeaux-Paris contest was the world's first motor race.

These events were important, because they reveal the ideas from which motor racing originated. Cars were then an entirely new form of transport, appealing to the adventurous private owner of means, and their ultimate purpose was to carry passengers from one locality to another. It appeared logical to try to discover which car could cover the ground in the shortest possible time and, as the initial race was a great success, this type of long-distance, town-to-town event continued for eight years, with average speeds rising steadily.

It was impossible for the courses to be guarded, because one of the main objects of the organizers was to make these races impressive by reason of their length.

MOTOR RACING AND RECORD BREAKING

In 1898 a race was run from Paris to Amsterdam and back, a distance of about 1,073 miles. In 1900 the first of the Gordon Bennett races was held, in which each nation nominated a team of cars; here, for the first time, machines ran under International racing colours, America being allotted red, because Italy had not yet entered the lists. The year 1901 saw the first appearance of true racing machines, as distinct from adapted touring cars, and an event was staged from Paris to Berlin. During the following year another great long-distance event was run between Paris and Vienna and, by this time, competitive motoring had produced machines which were very difficult to handle, because engine power had greatly increased.

Cars with 100 h.p. engines were appearing, capable of more than 80 m.p.h., and motor racing became hazardous; chassis design had not kept in step with the increase of speed. Then, in 1903, long-distance events over open and unguarded roads suddenly ended as the result of a race known as the Paris-Madrid.

Two hundred and sixteen cars, as well as fifty-nine motor-cycles, came to the start, which was again set at Versailles. The machines were to be sent away at intervals, the first being due to leave at half-past three in the morning, but its departure was delayed for fifteen minutes because it was still dark.

All night great crowds had been assembling, and spectators were already waiting along the course as far as Bordeaux, where the first day's racing was to end, the cars continuing to Madrid next morning. The whole affair was attended by extraordinary excitement on the part of spectators and competitors; the former were quite uncontrolled, and the latter had no thought

4 LAUTENSCHLAGER IN THE MERCÉDÈS WITH WHICH HE WON THE GRAND PRIX IN 1914

5 REPRESENTATIVE OF TRULY MODERN MOTOR RACING IS THE GRAND PRIX DE MONACO, HELD IN THE STREETS OF MONTE CARLO

other than to get the utmost possible speed from their machines.

In every village, after the race began, crowds pressed out to the road, to watch for the cars, running back only when a machine appeared. Each car raised a cloud of dust which obscured others that might be following close behind, and this resulted in a fatality soon after the start.

At a point forty-five miles outside Paris, a woman was struck by a car. At Chatellerault, a child ran into the road, and when a man attempted to rescue it both were hit by a machine, which then swerved into the crowd, injuring many of the spectators. Ninety miles farther on, another woman was struck while running across the road and, again, the car left the course, killing two spectators before it overturned, the driver and his mechanic being badly hurt.

This sort of thing was repeated again and again, and was accompanied by scores of accidents to the cars themselves. The machines touched speeds hitherto unknown and, along part of the road, one car was timed at above 90 m.p.h. Blinded by dust, drivers overturned their cars on corners. Two side-swiped as they ran side by side, and both were wrecked. Another ran into a dog, the impact deranging the steering so that the car dashed into trees, the driver being killed instantaneously. One vehicle went out of control while negotiating a level crossing, overturned and pinned the mechanic helplessly beneath, then caught fire.

The number of killed and injured was never accurately computed but, of two hundred and sixteen cars which left Paris, more than half were eliminated by smashes. Rumours of these disasters went ahead of the machines. Spectators became frightened as the leading cars drew nearer Bordeaux, so that people ran from the roadside and took shelter when the machines came in sight. The drivers who first reached Bordeaux stopped and waited anxiously for news; the men who followed them arrived unnerved by the fact that, every few miles, they had passed the scene of some ugly accident.

It was brought home to everyone concerned that motor racing had reached a dangerous pitch and, as a result, the event was abandoned. The winner, so far as the race had gone, was Gabriel on a 70 h.p. Mors; he had averaged 65·3 m.p.h., for three hundred and forty-two miles. This was the highest speed at which any event had yet been run, but his performance was overshadowed by the tragedies which had accompanied it.

The outcry which followed against motor racing made it evident that town-to-town events could never be held again, but the French authorities realized that racing must go on if cars were to be improved. It was then that the idea of 'closed' circuits was conceived—that is, courses from which normal traffic is diverted and where spectators are under proper control.

It is directly as a result of the lessons learned from the Paris-Madrid that road racing has taken on its modern form although, at first, circuits were far longer than those employed to-day. The future of motor racing became definite in 1906, when the Automobile Club of France organized the first real Grand Prix over a closed circuit at Le Mans, commencing a series which—run over various, but similar road courses—continued until 1914.

Races for the Grand Prix were distinguished by the fact that cars of one nation competed against those of another, as in the Gordon Bennett events. Only one team could enter from each country, which meant that

EARLY YEARS

manufacturers were striving for the honour of running, long before the race was actually held.

Each Grand Prix was fought out under circumstances of great excitement and intense international rivalry, and the last of these events was run off over a 23·5 miles' circuit near Lyons, in 1914. It was won by Lautenschlager on a Mercédès at an average speed of 65·83 m.p.h., for a total distance of 470 miles. The speed was very little above that reached in the Paris-Madrid race, but it was achieved with a completely different type of car. The Mercédès engine was better designed and was less than half the size of Gabriel's Mors, which indicates its technical improvement.

The last of the Grands Prix ended the days when teams of cars raced as representatives of their own countries. The war stopped all racing, and not until 1921 was it resumed seriously.

The sponsors of the world's first motor race, and of the Grands Prix, then organized the opening event of a series known as the *Grand Prix de l'Automobile Club de France* or, more simply, the French Grand Prix. In order to eliminate any possibility of cars developing into the monsters of pre-war days, engine size was limited to 3,000 c.c., and the initial race was won by an American driver, Jimmy Murphy. His Duesenberg averaged 78·1 m.p.h. over a distance of 321 miles, so that, although smaller, his machine was much faster than the huge old-style Grand Prix models.

In the following year, engine size was reduced to 2,000 c.c., and the French Grand Prix was won by a Fiat, which set up an average of 79·2 m.p.h., for 500 miles, making this event the fastest road race ever run, while the speed was achieved with one of the smallest racing cars ever built.

The regulations which forced the introduction of smaller engines had a double effect; they brought about a great improvement in design and, at the same time, they brought so rapid a decline in motor racing that the sport seemed likely to disappear.

The smaller, faster cars demanded extremely careful construction, involving much research and the use of special metals, all of which was so costly that manufacturers were unwilling to bear the expense. Racing was saved by the suggestion that sports machines—as distinct from true racing cars—should be matched against one another, and a twenty-four hours' Grand Prix d'Endurance was organized over a road circuit at Le Mans. This event proved so popular that it was widely imitated, and later produced a sudden swing back to the Paris-Madrid days.

In 1927 a race for sports cars—the Mille Miglia—was arranged in Italy. It was run over one thousand miles of quite unguarded roads, but people were now accustomed to motor-cars; the event roused the whole of Italy to enthusiasm, and did much to revive interest in motor racing generally.

About this time, it was discovered that sports machines —which had developed from former racing models—had so improved in performance that it was quite easy to turn them back into racing cars. Manufacturers began to turn out standard types of racing cars, based on their sports models, which could be bought at a reasonable price by enthusiasts. This, accompanied by increased public interest, brought a resuscitation of real Grand Prix events, aided by the fact that a number of motor-racing tracks were opening.

Except at Brooklands, and at the Indianapolis Speedway

6 CARS BEING EXAMINED BY THE SCRUTINEERS AT BRESCIA, ON THE DAY BEFORE THE MILLE MIGLIA

7 THE GRANDSTAND AND ENCLOSURES USED FOR THE TRIPOLI GRAND PRIX, THE WORLD'S FASTEST ROAD RACE

EARLY YEARS

in America, all racing had taken place upon ordinary roads. This dislocated local traffic, but a track could be used at any time, a fact which had obvious advantages. An autodrome was opened at Linas-Montlhèry, near Paris, and another was built at Miramas, near Marseilles. The Italians constructed Monza Speedway, close to Milan, and the Germans built the largest track in the world and called it the Nurburg Ring.

Each of these special courses differed in essential features. Monza permitted very high speeds, but the track had many dangerous bends. Miramas was simply a flat, three-mile circle of concrete. The Linas-Montlhèry autodrome was virtually a gigantic bowl, and so well surfaced that it became recognized as the fastest track in the world and, for this reason, soon formed a centre for record breaking. The German track was designed to reproduce features of a road.

After 1927 the revival of motor racing was very rapid. Many new events were introduced, and in 1929 an altogether unusual type of race was organized. The Automobile Club de Monaco issued regulations for a race to be held through the streets of the Principality, and it proved to be the most spectacular that the world has yet known. The roar of fast machines in the streets, the excitement of spectators at every window and vantage point, the constant passing of cars as they returned about the short course, were so impressive that similar events were organized in other towns.

As the seasons passed motor racing, which had once seemed likely to deteriorate until it attracted only an initiated minority, broadened its interest until, in the present year, its very popularity has enforced a variety which is astonishing.

Races are now run over normal roads, and over prepared road circuits which, in some cases, have taken on the appearance of special tracks. There are events along lonely sand beaches, and through the streets of populous towns. Speed trials are held up steep hills, over mountain passes, and along new, special motor highways. There are races on cinder-surfaced courses and, in winter time, over frozen lakes and snowbound roads. Cars run on tracks paved with concrete, with bricks, or with normal road surfacing, while record breaking has reached such a pitch that the world has been scoured for suitable natural courses which will permit specially built machines to reach their maximum pace.

Speeds have increased and, forty years after the first of all races, a new peak was reached in the Grand Prix of Tripoli. This road race in North Africa was run off over a distance of 325 miles, and in 1935 it was won by Rudolf Caracciola at an average of 123·03 m.p.h., the greatest speed yet attained in a road event.

In some aspects, motor racing may appear simply as an exciting sport, but its primary object is the betterment of cars as a whole. It may be said that every improvement in the actual efficiency of motor vehicles has emanated from motor racing.

Cars have changed and this has brought a change in the men who handle them. The majority of pioneer drivers were big and muscular, because the work required real physical strength. They contrast greatly with such a man as Tazio Nuvolari, one of the finest of modern race drivers. He is slight of build, and weighs barely a hundred and thirty pounds, which suggests that controlling the high-speed machine of to-day demands quick nervous reaction and mental swiftness rather than physique.

8 RACING OVER SAND AT SKEGNESS, LINCOLNSHIRE

9 RACING OVER ICE, IN SWEDEN

10 RUDOLF CARACCIOLA, WITH A MERCÉDÈS-BENZ, CLEARING A DANGEROUS CURVE ON THE MONZA TRACK

11 BROOKLANDS' BIGGEST CAR. THE NAPIER-RAILTON, PHOTOGRAPHED AT MONTLHÈRY DURING PRACTICE FOR RECORD ATTEMPTS

EARLY YEARS

The pace of a modern racing car is very high. Undoubtedly speeds will go still higher, but only as cars are designed to achieve it with safety. These same safety features must, when applied to normal machines, be to the benefit of all who drive them.

That is why motor racing goes on. It is a consistent and continuous effort to win still more knowledge, and a survey of the events which form the sport may help to give a better understanding of the drivers and of their cars.

CHAPTER II

ROAD RACING

Motor racing is admittedly the most dangerous of all sports, and road racing is the most exacting of its many forms.

Success demands certain characteristics in a driver. Coolness is a first essential, and with this he must combine considerable dash and fighting spirit. He needs real courage, as distinct from the recklessness which invites trouble, while it is easy to appreciate that his life depends upon the possession of absolutely exact judgment.

The need for these qualities becomes apparent in such an event as the Grand Prix de la Marne, one of the most representative of modern road races. It is a run just outside Reims, over a circuit rather less than five miles in length, the nature of which makes it the fastest road course in Europe.

As the prize-money amounts to considerably more than three thousand pounds, the event attracts the finest drivers on the Continent, and the race is very keen from the outset, invariably opening with a fierce fight for leadership before the first corner is reached. This is a right-angle turn lying about a mile from the start, and it is approached by a road barely thirty feet in width, which bends twice and ends in a downward gradient to the corner. In the 1934 race, the fourteen competing cars were all capable of at least 140 m.p.h., and the spectacle of the machines, when they left at the fall of the flag, racing for the first turn, was one which roused the huge crowd lining the road to real excitement.

12 CARACCIOLA'S MERCÉDÈS LEADING IN THE 1934 COPPA ACERBO, HELD OVER THE VERY FAST PESCARA CIRCUIT, ITALY

13 THE OPENING OF THE GRAND PRIX DE LA MARNE, HELD OUTSIDE REIMS, OVER THE FASTEST EUROPEAN ROAD CIRCUIT

ROAD RACING

Guy Moll—a twenty-four-year-old driver from Algiers—led the way, the rest hard on his tail, spread out across the road, passing and repassing one another, engines roaring in gear and open exhausts howling. A driver requires courage to remain with the rest when cars are bunched in this way. He has to watch the machines ahead and on either side, knowing that a single slip or fault on the part of any man will involve others.

Clear of that first corner on the Reims circuit, the road rises, then sweeps through a series of bends to another right-angle turn, which brings the circuit on to a straight which runs downhill for a full mile, then rises gently in an approach to Thillois corner—almost a hairpin turn. During the race, the fastest cars touch above 150 m.p.h. towards the end of this straight, but any attempt to go through the Thillois turn at much more than 40 m.p.h. will result in a skid. Such a skid involves the risk of being rammed by following machines, or the car may slide outwards and hit the wire-bound trusses of straw placed to guard spectators; either contingency would result in damage, almost inevitably bringing retirement from the race.

Travelling at 150 m.p.h., a driver has to place his car in readiness for the turn, then brake down to 40 m.p.h. and, at the same time, change gear in order to make the utmost possible use of his acceleration from the corner. If a driver loses one-fifth of a second on this—or any other—turn, his rivals gain nearly ten yards because, right from the start of this race, machines lap at rather more than 90 m.p.h.

In 1934 the opening lap ended with Achille Varzi—an Italian driver—about five yards in front of Guy Moll, on whose tail were Tazio Nuvolari and Louis Chiron; ten yards farther in rear were two other cars. The close placing of these six leading machines indicates how evenly matched were men and cars; at the end of this first lap of five miles, there was not one second of difference between them. Those six cars went through every bend and every corner in a bunch, providing one of the outstanding spectacles in motor racing. At the finish of the second lap, their positions had not changed except that Nuvolari, by gaining half a second somewhere at the back of the course, had jumped in front of Moll.

It was impossible that such effort could be long sustained by men and machines and, with the third lap, Varzi drew ahead, while the rest strung out, but the illustration does demonstrate the fact that it is sheer skill and not recklessness which counts in road racing. The least weakening, or the slightest lack of crisp and definite action on some difficult part of the course, means the displacement of a car by another handled with more dash.

The ability necessary to run successfully in important Grands Prix can usually be acquired only by constant driving in lesser events, coupled with some natural aptitude. Yet, occasionally, a driver will appear so gifted that, with very little experience, he can challenge men who have years of racing experience behind them. Such a man is Whitney Straight, the young American who made his debut in Grands Prix at Reims in 1933. Formerly, he had engaged in little other than Brooklands track events, yet he handled his machine with such skill that, although he failed to finish the race, his impressive performance made him a favourite with the spectators when he ran again in 1934.

Another driver of similar merit was Guy Moll, who eventually took second place in the Grand Prix de la

Marne of 1934. Two years earlier he had been a complete novice, but within twelve months he was rivalling the most famous of drivers. His style was always faultlessly cool and skilful, but within five weeks of the Reims event he became a victim of bad racing luck. Driving on the Pescara circuit, in Italy, holding second place and challenging the leader, he had passed another machine when his car skidded outwards. Moll was then on the fastest part of the circuit, travelling downhill at a speed approaching 160 m.p.h., and he slid off the edge of the road into a shallow ditch. He struggled to bring the machine back to the course, but the car turned over and he was flung out, the machine leaping high into the air and turning upside down. Moll was killed instantaneously, and motor racing was robbed of a man who would almost certainly have made history.

As an indication of the fact that such a mishap can happen to the most experienced of drivers, Louis Chiron —who has been racing for over ten years without accident—skidded in the Belgian Grand Prix three weeks before Moll's crash, and his car went on to the grass. Chiron had straightened out, when one rear wheel hit a rock at the roadside, and the machine turned completely over. Fortunately, Chiron was thrown clear and was so little hurt that he was able to walk back to the replenishment pits.

A driver's personal reactions during any race are somewhat unusual, and the more difficult the event, the less clear is his recollection of its details.

He rides half deafened by the noise of his engine and the sound of his exhaust. As the laps run out, his cockpit grows very hot, while he becomes bruised and stiff under the hammering that he receives from the hard springs.

Constant gear-changing, and the necessity for maintaining a considerable grip on the steering wheel, fatigue his wrists and forearms. The heat of the sun probably adds to his discomfort, while particles of gritty dust chafe his neck and parch his mouth.

A driver has little opportunity, however, to appreciate these physical discomforts, unless the pace of the race slackens. His entire attention is devoted to his car and the fight which he is making. Over every mile of the race, he must press his machine to as near the limit of its performance as he dare, watching for his braking points before every turn, positioning his car for each bend and, on the straights, glancing at his instruments to make certain that all is well.

Apart from all this, he must be prepared to cope with any failure of his machine or any untoward incident, such as occurred in the 1934 Reims race, when Nuvolari was passing the grandstand at above 120 m.p.h. and the tread stripped from one rear tyre. Fragments of torn rubber were hurled high into the air, and the machine started to skid, but the Italian countered this instantly, straightened and continued at the same speed, completing another lap before he stopped to change the wheel. He did not know that the tyre was about to give out; it was his own mental swiftness, his ability to bring innate skill immediately to his aid, that prevented the skid developing into a broadside slide which, at such pace, might have ended in disaster.

Although the Grand Prix de la Marne is outstanding, history and tradition make the French Grand Prix the most important event in the international calendar, and it is now a road race of a quite different order from that at Reims. At one time it was run off on a variety of

14 THESE THREE ALFA-ROMEOS WERE TRAVELLING AT ABOUT 140 M.P.H. DURING THE OPENING LAP OF THE GRAND PRIX DE LA MARNE IN 1934. LOUIS CHIRON LEADS FROM ACHILLE VARZI AND GUY MOLL.

15 THE MERCÉDÈS, WITH RUDOLF CARACCIOLA AT THE WHEEL, WHICH WON THE 1935 GRAND PRIX OF TRIPOLI

16 SPECTATORS AT THE GRAND PRIX DE TUNISIE

courses, usually near big towns: Tours, Strasbourg, Lyons. Recently, however, the artificial road circuit attached to the Linas-Montlhèry autodrome, south-west of Paris, has come to be regarded as the accepted setting for this event, which is a true successor to the old Grands Prix.

The Montlhèry track stands on a high ridge, and the course runs along its summit, consisting of two roads which, for all practical purposes, are parallel. The circuit is artificial in the sense that it is not normally used as a highway; it was planned solely for road racing, and was designed to bring out the best in competing cars and drivers.

Some sections are altogether more sinuous than the Reims course, with the result that the highest average lap speed ever set up at Montlhèry in the French Grand Prix is 91·9 m.p.h. This was achieved by Louis Chiron in 1934, and the very strenuous nature of the race is indicated by the fact that, of the thirteen starters, only three cars actually completed the event. The reason for these retirements may become clear if the course itself is considered.

The circuit starts from the southern side of the Montlhèry track, where a tarred road opens from the concrete, running straight and level for almost a mile, then making a curve which can just be taken flat out. It requires considerable nerve to go through this bend with the throttle wide open, and it leads to another mile of straight which ends in a very steep, abrupt dip set just at the point where brakes must be used if machines are safely to negotiate what are known as the Couard Bends.

The first of these bends is at the summit of a short upgrade, forming a flat, concrete-surfaced turn which can be very treacherous during wet weather. Two more bends lead into a short falling straight which comes so abruptly that cars invariably leave the ground as they enter it, wheels momentarily spinning in thin air. At the bottom of the slope is a sharp, falling turn to the left; within the quarter of a mile comes a hairpin turn beyond which, in barely another quarter-mile, is another left-hand corner, followed by a series of four curves. This point —Les Biscornes—forms the eastern extremity of the course and brings the machines on to the return road.

The two miles before Les Biscornes incorporate nine corners of varying severity, and one hairpin turn; engine and gear-box have no respite on this stretch, while the driver is swung from side to side in his cockpit, particularly on the final four turns at Les Biscornes. Each of these, although 'blind,' can be taken flat out in third gear by a good driver, and once around them the return road begins with a switchback straight of over a mile, ending in a climbing turn through woods at Forêt Corner.

There are more bends in the next half-mile, after which the course runs parallel with the outward road until it nears the actual track. Here a swinging corner leads to another hairpin, and the circuit then re-enters the autodrome on the north side. Machines run around the western banking, which is extremely high and steep, with a sheer drop on the far side. They then dive from this to the flat in front of the grandstands—completing the lap—and rush for the entrance to the road section which, to a racing man, appears no more than a very narrow throat between concrete walls, with the tarred highway stretching beyond it.

In summer, the course is very pleasant in appearance. Wild flowers bloom beside tinted sandbanks and stretches of heather grow near the slopes, with bushes and trees forming a green background. The circuit is worthy of

17 THE FLAG HAS JUST FALLEN TO START THESE CARS IN THE FRENCH GRAND PRIX AT LINAS-MONTLHÉRY. NO. 8 IS A MERCÉDÈS-BENZ DRIVEN BY CARACCIOLA, AND NO. 6 IS AN ALFA-ROMEO WITH VARZI AT THE WHEEL

18 CONDITIONS IN THE GRAND PRIX OF ALGIERS ARE DEMONSTRATED BY THIS PHOTOGRAPH OF SPORTS MACHINES ENGAGED IN A RACE PRELIMINARY TO THE EVENT FOR GRAND PRIX CARS

19 HANS VON STUCK TAKING HIS AUTO-UNION DOWN A STRAIGHT OF THE LINAS-MONTLHÈRY ROAD CIRCUIT IN THE FRENCH GRAND PRIX OF 1934

ROAD RACING

the French Grand Prix, and the road has everywhere been designed to offer the maximum of safety for fast-moving machines. Largely because of this, it is not often that the race is marred by accident. When cars are in the hands of the best road-racing drivers in the world, using a course planned for their work, there is little room for those errors of judgment which, usually, are behind a crash.

Conversely, one of the attractions of road racing lies in the fact that machines have to face the hazards which an existing road may hold. This occurs at Reims, and is again repeated on such a course as the Ards Circuit in Ulster, over which the Tourist Trophy race is run.

This latter event is not for true racing cars. It forms the modern counterpart of events in which pioneers of the sport engaged. They drove ordinary machines, and the T.T. is for sports models, the performance of which has been enhanced only in a limited degree, and in accordance with the regulations governing the race. The Tourist Trophy was not instituted with the object of improving racing machines, but was intended to develop 'touring' cars, as the name implies, and every machine must be in normal production by its manufacturer.

The circuit is a difficult one, yet speeds reached in the T.T. compare in a surprising way with those of outstanding events for stripped racing machines. The 1934 French Grand Prix was won by an Alfa-Romeo at 85 m.p.h., over a distance of 315 miles; the Tourist Trophy race of the same year was won by an M.G. Magnette at 74·6 m.p.h., over a race distance of 478 miles. This car was not supercharged, its engine was much less than half the size of that of the Alfa-Romeo, while it had to travel half as far again to win the race, running over a natural road circuit. Still further, it was a standard sports machine, while the Alfa-Romeo was a single-seater racing car. In spite of this, the M.G. was barely 10 m.p.h. slower.

The fact that the Tourist Trophy event can evoke such excellent performance stresses the value of the race. Its spectacular appeal may be less than that of a Continental Grand Prix, but it has a very sporting element. The prizes offered are not high and, for this reason, of late years, the majority of drivers are men who have competed only at Brooklands and in various lesser events.

Usually a large number of cars start and, as they are of various sizes, the race is run under a handicap, while it invariably offers exciting incident to the half-million spectators who come to watch.

In 1934 one car, taken too fast into a corner, shot up a bank and leaped over a hedge, another skidded unhappily into a ditch and a third caught fire. The race itself was marked by a tremendous duel, when two of the fastest cars constantly lapped within close reach of one another, passing and re-passing until tyre trouble obliged one to stop. The conclusion was formed by a desperate effort on part of the driver of a Rolls-Bentley, in second place, to overtake the leader; he failed by the very narrow margin of seventeen seconds.

The course employed for the T.T. is long, measuring 13·6 miles, but this is suitable to the large field and the nature of the race itself. The present tendency is, generally, to shorten a road circuit, in order that cars may pass more frequently, increasing the interest for spectators.

It is peculiar that each road race seems to take on the character of the circuit over which it is run. The Circuito

20 AN UNUSUAL VIEW THROUGH A SHOP WINDOW OF AN M.G. CAR RACING ACROSS NEWTOWNARDS SQUARE DURING A TOURIST TROPHY RACE

21 RACING ON THE DONINGTON PARK CIRCUIT, LEICESTERSHIRE, THE ONLY ROAD-TYPE COURSE IN ENGLAND

22 'CHARLEY' DODSON CROSSING THE FINISHING LINE WITH AN M.G. MAGNETTE, WINNING THE 1934 TOURIST TROPHY RACE

ROAD RACING

Bordino, a race held at the edge of Alessandria, Italy, is usually a grim and desperate affair; the course itself is dull, featureless, and quite flat, and where it runs through part of the town it has drab surroundings.

Rain helped to make the circuit still less pleasant when the last race was held. One machine charged into the crowd, and another rammed a wall, overturning and bursting into flames. On one of the two bridges which the course traverses, a car went out of control, smashing into the iron railings with such force that the driver was flung across the road, to be killed when he struck more railings opposite the wreckage of his car.

Hardly a couple of hundred yards beyond this point, Tazio Nuvolari slid off the road and overturned in a ditch close to the edge of the course. He fractured his leg, and received first-aid on the footpath while other machines raced past.

The majority of road circuits—and over twenty are employed in the course of the racing season—are more pleasant, and one of the finest is that at St. Gaudens, in the south of France and over which the Grand Prix de Comminges is run. It has a unique setting, and is placed at the base of the Pyrenees, with a grandstand cut out of the side of a hill, overlooking the valley which is traversed by the road.

Many drivers are of the opinion that this is the most sporting course of all, and the race invariably proves to be an excellent event. The circuit is seven miles in length, and contains every type of bend and corner that can be found, with the exception of a hairpin. From the starting-point at the top of the hill, by the grandstand, cars descend a steep slope which brings them, through another corner, to a long stretch formed by a succession of very fast bends. This ends in two curves which return the machines to a magnificent two-mile straight, at the finish of which they run up the hill to the grandstand again.

Whitney Straight drove here in 1934, making so splendid a start at the fall of the flag that he leaped into the lead and retained it for five laps. He was then passed by an Italian, Franco Comotti, who broke the lap record with 96 m.p.h. In view of the nature of the circuit, such speed is extraordinarily high, but it was afterwards beaten by Marcel Lehoux who covered the course at 97·8 m.p.h. The event ended in a victory for Comotti at an average of 93 m.p.h., Whitney Straight running into third place. The winner's speed would appear to challenge the title of the Reims circuit as the fastest in Europe, but the Grand Prix de Comminges was run over only two hundred and forty miles, instead of three hundred.

A significant feature of the Comminges race is that it was won by a member of what is known as the *scuderia* Ferrari. This Italian term finds its equivalent in the French *équipe*, or our own 'stable,' and the formation of such teams amongst racing men is a development of very recent years. A *scuderia* is a combination of drivers banded together for the racing season, and sometimes making use of one *marque* of car only—the Ferrari stable use Alfa-Romeo machines—and working under a mutual agreement concerning any prize-money they may win.

Formerly, teams running in a race consisted of machines entered by the manufacturer of the cars, who selected his drivers, generally retaining them for the season. Such a plan is very costly because, in addition to building the cars, a manufacturer has to finance their preparation for a race, and provide for the expenses which accompany any event.

Although the modern *scuderia* generally works in close liaison with the manufacturers whose cars the drivers handle, each forms a quite independent unit. The Ferrari *scuderia* has its own badge—a yellow shield, bearing the figure of a horse—and was one of the first to be formed. Many other such teams exist, some of which embody drivers who find that mutual assistance is less expensive than driving as what the French term an *indépendent*.

It is the creation of these stables, and the rivalry between them, which has helped to sustain road racing. Usually the drivers compete as a team, working in unison to break up any opposition but, where the dates of events clash, a driver may run alone as a representative of his stable.

In the Grand Prix de Comminges, Lehoux and Comotti drove for the *scuderia* Ferrari on the day that other members of this stable were engaged in the Swiss Grand Prix, over four hundred miles away. In this event the Ferrari drivers were Chiron, Varzi, and Count Trossi; they proved unsuccessful, possibly because the Swiss race was held towards the close of the season, and many months of hard racing may have told upon their ability. They had to face very strong opposition, but Varzi—who took fourth place—was less than two minutes behind the winner, with Chiron only forty seconds farther back.

If the race, which was over three hundred miles, had been earlier in the season, the probability is that these two drivers would have been much faster. On the other hand, the winner of the event might have been able to produce still more speed, and would have held them off in any case, but the circumstances do offer an indication of an aspect of modern motor racing which is not always appreciated.

MOTOR RACING AND RECORD BREAKING

The international calendar is very crowded, and every Sunday brings some important race; the short intervals between them offer scant respite. It is sometimes the case that a man has to be lifted from his machine at the end of a road event; reserves of nervous energy sustain him until the race reaches its conclusion, then exhaustion follows. The intense concentration which driving entails, and which cannot be broken even for the fraction of a second, takes its toll. A man in excellent physical condition recovers very rapidly, but in time the keenness of his ability must be blunted, and it is then that he finds himself slower than he should be, tiring more easily. That, of course, happens in any sport, but it applies particularly to road racing.

Just as a successful driver must possess essential qualities, so a car must have certain features. It must be very stable, in order to hold the road at high speed, and it is vital that it should have very precise steering; this means a great deal to a driver who is cornering fast, with his machine close to the skidding point. Brakes are of vital importance, because a man needs to hold his speed until the last possible moment in approaching a turn.

These features have been brought to a high degree of perfection solely as a result of competitive motoring, and road racing develops just those things which are essential in a production car. Although it is obvious that the ordinary driver has no wish to travel at a pace approaching 150 m.p.h., the fact remains that the design which enables a racing machine to remain on the road at this speed does, when adapted to a normal vehicle, help that car to become so much safer.

In this lies the value of road racing, but the very

23 IMMEDIATELY BEFORE THE START OF THE GRAND PRIX OF CZECHOSLOVAKIA

24 THE OPENING OF THE PENYA RHIN GRAND PRIX, BARCELONA

25 ON THE LASARTE CIRCUIT NEAR SAN SEBASTIAN DURING THE SPANISH GRAND PRIX

demands of road circuits involve certain limitations and restricting factors. A car can never be driven at the absolute limit of its possible speed, because of the nature of the course; its hill-climbing capabilities cannot be rigorously tested, because the inclusion of steep gradients would slow cars and rob an event of its interest for spectators. So, while road racing remains as the supreme test of a car, the development of certain features of design is left to other forms of the sport.

CHAPTER III

TRACK RACING

THE advantage of a course specially built for motor racing is that it may be used at any time, and a track is generally constructed with the object of permitting cars to travel as fast as possible; for this reason, any bends made necessary in the design of the course are usually struck at a wide radius, and are banked.

The tendency of track racing is to develop machines in which everything is sacrificed to maximum speed. The driver's comfort is of minor importance; in some cars he often sits on no more than an inch-thick pad of rubber placed over a metal seat. Effective brakes are very often dispensed with because they are not normally required until a race has ended, when there is usually plenty of distance in which to stop the machine. Even visibility is often sacrificed in order to secure better streamlining, and a driver's seat may be so placed that the nearest point that he can see, immediately in front of the car, may be as much as thirty or forty yards ahead.

The designer of a car for track work concerns himself with speed, and with speed only. He works incessantly to obtain more and more power from his engine and, at the same time, he has to develop the machine's transmission in order that it may translate this power into terms of speed. This alone indicates that every track is something of a laboratory, a place where certain essential features of a car may be tested and tried to the utmost. The knowledge thus secured is applied to road racing and other forms of competitive

26 LIGHT AND SHADOW ON THE PATCHED CONCRETE OF BROOKLANDS

27 STALLED BY ITS DRIVER AT THE FALL OF THE FLAG, THIS CAR HAS BEEN PUSH-STARTED BY MECHANICS

motoring which, in their turn, develop other characteristics of the car.

Track work is a distinct phase of motor racing, demanding its own tactics. The cars are altogether more delicate than machines built for the road, and the judgment required by the drivers is of a different order. In a long-distance track race, it is seldom that the men who make the pace at the outset are amongst the leaders at the finish, and many an event has been won by a car which has run at several miles an hour below its true maximum speed.

A driver's greatest difficulty is to handle his machine with restraint. He has an open course before him, and there is nothing to prevent his employing full throttle from start to finish, except that he knows his engine might not stand the strain. He has, therefore, to drive at such a speed as to keep his engine revolutions below danger-point, and to maintain that speed even though other cars may leave him behind. Only when the issue of the race becomes clear, when he sees that victory may be gained by driving flat out, dare he travel at full throttle, matching the chance of winning against the possibility of 'blowing up' his engine and retiring from the event altogether.

Every track provides its own limitations to speed, because all such artificial courses must necessarily take on a form approximating to a circle, and the angle of the banking automatically reduces the possible rate of travel. There are machines in existence capable of maximum speeds which are altogether too high for any track that has yet been built; the highest lap speed ever recorded on a banked motor course—up to the end of 1934—is 147·79 m.p.h., which was attained on the Linas-Montlhéry circuit. In a short, straightaway dash, 200 m.p.h.

has been exceeded on the road, but this pace could not be duplicated at Montlhèry, and any attempt to reach it would probably result in the machine flying over the top of the banking.

Although every existing track has a limit at which a car can travel around it, this is due only to its size, shape, and design; there would be no theoretical difficulty at all in the actual construction of a course on which cars could reach four or even five miles a minute.

The first motor-racing track ever built was the Brooklands Motor Course, at Weybridge, in Surrey, which was opened on June 17th, 1907, the first race being held there three weeks later. It cost £150,000 to construct, and was built because road racing was, and still is, not permitted in England; a circuit of some sort seemed very desirable if the motor industry was to be given a fair opportunity against foreign competition.

Brooklands is oviform, with a lap length of 2 miles 1,350 yards; the track is everywhere at least one hundred feet wide, and is surfaced with concrete. Although opened over a quarter of a century ago, and at a time when it was not expected that cars would ever travel at much above 120 m.p.h., the track is used more than any of those which followed it, and forms the setting for the world's fastest long-distance race. This is the five hundred miles event organized by the British Racing Drivers' Club, which has been won at a speed of 118 m.p.h.

As with other tracks, a driver is favoured in a race if he knows Brooklands well, because, for the very fast cars, its shape does not permit sustained speed all the way round. It has one relatively short curve, with banking so steep that a man cannot climb it on foot,

28 GETTING AWAY AT THE START OF AN EVENT ON THE AVUS TRACK, BERLIN

29 IN THE RAIN AT BROOKLANDS. THIS BUGATTI WAS TRAVELLING AT 125 M.P.H. ALONG THE 'RAILWAY' STRAIGHT

30 AN AERIAL VIEW OF INDIANAPOLIS SPEEDWAY. ONE LAP HAD BEEN COVERED WHEN THIS PHOTOGRAPH WAS SECURED, BUT THE CARS ARE STILL BUNCHED AS THEY PASS THE STANDS

and this leads on to what is known as the 'railway straight.' This is about half a mile in length, and enters the very long Byfleet curve, where the banking is not so high. From this, cars drop to another short straight with a reverse curve, and then run on to the steep banking again.

The track surface is rough, and the course itself has features which make Brooklands hard on a car; machines which have performed successfully on other circuits frequently fail to stand up to the strain which this track can impose. The circuit, too, is so large that straight-away races have a tendency to become monotonous, not only for drivers but for spectators as well; the majority of important events now held there are run over courses so contrived that they imitate road conditions, bends being formed from sandbags and straw bales, lines of flags and wattle hurdles, creating corners which offer hazards similar to those on a normal road circuit.

Typical of such races is that held for the British Empire Trophy; in 1935 a course was arranged which included two difficult turns, with an S-bend set in the railway straight and sharp hairpin bend placed a half-mile farther on. This event was close-fought and dramatic, although it was neither a true road race nor a true track event. If Brooklands, however, were limited to its original conception, and events were run only over the cleared outer circuit, the effect would not be good; it is the adaptability of the authorities at the track which has enabled Brooklands to retain its position as the most active course in the world. In order to capture public interest, a few years ago 'mountain' races were introduced, where a relatively short lap just over a mile long is used, the course running round the 'members' hill,' or 'mountain,' and including two sharp corners.

Incidentally, the general atmosphere at England's only track is unique. The course is set in pine woods, and its centre is occupied by an aerodrome. Clustered about the paddock are garages and tuning sheds, beyond which lie open meadows where, at times, cows browse within a few yards of cars passing at 140 m.p.h.

Completely different from Brooklands is the Indianapolis Speedway, which was the second track to be built. This American course was opened in August 1909 and is square in shape, with a length of two and a half miles, the four corners being only moderately banked. Originally, the track was surfaced with macadam, but this broke up during early races and was replaced by brick paving. Over three million bricks were employed in this work, and the surface has remained virtually the same throughout the whole of the life of the track; its only defect is that, in the event of rain, the course becomes dangerously slippery.

Only one race is held in each year at Indianapolis. This takes place at the end of May, and involves the largest prize-money offered for any motor event; the race is preceded by eliminating tests, which require cars to cover ten laps of the course at an average speed in excess of 100 m.p.h. Competing drivers are usually drawn from those who run in events on dirt tracks scattered about the country; although some years ago machines were sent across from Europe to take part, and met with success, such entries are infrequent.

The four corners present the chief difficulty at Indianapolis, where speeds have become so high that the race requires machines which, to a great extent, have been specially designed for the circuit. The fastest lap ever set up on the track was at 124·01 m.p.h., by Leon Duray on a Miller, while the pace which can be attained by skilled drivers is indicated by the average of 119 m.p.h. achieved by Kelly Petillo in the eliminating trials before the 1934 race, which proved to be a typical Indianapolis event.

First prize amounted to about six thousand pounds, while the driver who led at the end of each lap—two hundred laps made the total for the race—received an award of five pounds. This system of awarding prize-money for lap leadership ensures every driver doing his utmost to get ahead, because, even if he does not win, he can gain a substantial reward if he manages to retain the lead for even a short time.

The event was heralded by a parade of a thousand bandsmen, while a crowd of 150,000 gathered. The race was very fast, and was characterized by a daring on the part of the drivers which, in some cases, amounted almost to desperation. At the end of twenty laps when the leader was averaging 106 m.p.h., a car skidded to the top of the banking on a curve and crashed through the safety fence, while another suddenly spun round on the course and was rammed by a machine which followed close behind. Immediately afterwards, yet another car skidded near the scene of the first crash, struck the guard rail, and somersaulted wildly—yet the only injury resulting from these high-speed smashes was a broken wrist, sustained by the first driver to leave the track.

Forty laps later, when the pace had eased to 105 m.p.h., a car broke its steering and dived to the inside of the course. Shortly afterwards, two more machines came into contact with the guard rail on a curve. This brought the total up to seven crashes inside the first one hundred and fifty miles, but none was marked by serious consequences, and the race was won by Bill Cummings, who averaged 104·8 m.p.h.

American motor racing has been bred from events on cinder-surfaced courses and what are known as 'board' tracks. The latter are steeply banked courses, surfaced with planking, usually with a lap distance of about one mile. On so smooth a course, very high speeds can be obtained, and they produced machines in which everything gave place to lightness and great engine power. Such events were extremely spectacular, the cars being piloted by men inured to travelling over the boards at anything up to 140 m.p.h., riding dangerously close to rival machines.

The majority of these tracks now stand disused, as a result of the effect of the weather upon their 'woodwork.' Some of them have been the settings for disastrous accidents, and an extraordinary series of smashes occurred during a two hundred miles event at Rockingham Speedway. Shortly after the start, a car burst a tyre at 130 m.p.h., somersaulted three times and pinned the driver beneath its wreckage. Ten minutes later another car hit the retaining wall at the upper edge of the banking, leaped into the air and rolled down towards the inside of the course. Three following machines, in trying to avoid the wreck, cannoned into one another and were put out of the race. Only a few minutes later, another car ran out of control and hit the retaining wall, losing its front axle. The officials stopped the race at this point, when barely fifty miles had been covered.

An even worse series of accidents occurred at Altoona Speedway, another board track. Here, again, a car skidded into the retaining wall and slid across the course. Six machines were close behind it, and the leader struck the falling car. The other five either piled into the wreckage or rammed one another in trying to avoid it.

31 THE LINE-UP FOR THE START OF THE INDIANAPOLIS FIVE HUNDRED MILES RACE

32 AT CULVER CITY SPEEDWAY, A CALIFORNIA BOARD TRACK. THESE CARS WERE COMPETING IN A 250-MILES EVENT

TRACK RACING

Board-track racing obviously required very steady nerves and great coolness, and the same is true of dirt-track events, while the Indianapolis race—where very high speeds are demanded, combined with extremely clever work on the corners—always produces extraordinarily skilful driving.

In a different degree, these same essentials are necessary for success on the track which was the third to be completed. This is the Avus course, just outside Berlin. This German track was conceived in the year that Brooklands was first opened, but work was not begun until four years later. It was abandoned during the war, but was taken up again in 1921, the course being completed the next year.

In shape it is peculiar, consisting of two roads, running parallel, each six miles in length and joined at either end by two abrupt curves. This design was followed as a result of a doubt concerning the financial success of a motor-racing track; the organizing company decided that the course should be one which would also serve as a special motor road. The controlling company is known as *Automobil-Verkehrs-und-Uebungs-Strasse*—the Automobile Testing and Trials Road company—and its initials, A.V.U.S., name the track.

The twin roads are absolutely straight and are more or less flat, separated by a strip of grass; since each road is six miles in length, very high speeds can be attained.

The Avus track has seen the closest finish in the history of motor racing. In 1933 Achille Varzi won the Avus International race at an average speed of 128·5 m.p.h., over 183 miles, finishing one-tenth of a second in front of the car which followed him home, while two other machines dead-heated for third place. The design of the Avus course requires a car which can reach high speed very quickly and which, at the same time, will not slide on the two sharp curves. Driving is largely a matter of successfully negotiating the turns, and bringing the car to top speed again along the following straights. Remarkable world's records were established here during 1934 by Hans von Stuck, driving a German Auto-Union car, who averaged 152·17 m.p.h. for 100 kms. and captured the much coveted world's hour record at over 134 m.p.h. This feat, following upon an earlier successful attack on the world's hour record by Count Czaykowski at the same track, has given rise to the belief that Avus, in spite of its design, is now the best place in Europe for an attack on the medium-distance world's records.

This view has been lent further support by the fact that the world's fastest race was run off there in May 1935. This was the Avus Grand Prix, which was held in a series of two heats and a final event, the latter being over ten laps, equivalent to a distance of 122 miles. This was won by Luigi Fagioli, driving a Mercédès-Benz, at the amazing speed of 148·2 m.p.h. The speed of Louis Chiron's Auto-Union, which gained second place was 143·5 m.p.h., and Achille Varzi, who drove a similar car, averaged 141·6 m.p.h. and was placed third.

During the Grand Prix, Hans von Stuck's Auto-Union was estimated to have touched 185 m.p.h. along the straights, while he put in a lap at 163 m.p.h., but such speed involved delays from tyre troubles and he finished fourth in an event which has set a new mark in motor-racing history.

An altogether different type of course from that at Avus is one which was opened in September 1922 at

33 THE START OF A RACE AT AVUS. THE TWIN STRAIGHTS WHICH FORM THIS TRACK ARE CLEARLY SHOWN

34 TWO AUTO-UNION MACHINES TRAVELLING IN REVERSE DIRECTION ALONG THE DOUBLE STRAIGHT AT MONZA DURING THE 1934 ITALIAN GRAND PRIX

Monza, about ten miles from Milan, a circuit which was constructed in royal parkland, the actual work occupying only sixteen weeks. The track is splendidly organized, having no less than thirteen grandstands set beside the main straight, while the replenishment pits opposite are unusually efficient and neat. With the increase of speeds since the course was first opened, various precautions have been taken towards making the circuit safe, including a concrete retaining wall between the straight and the enclosure in front of the grandstand.

The Monza Speedway was planned to incorporate many features of an ordinary road. It is peculiar in design, consisting of a lozenge-shaped section with an outer circuit attached, the total length being six and a quarter miles. It has two excellent straights, each three-quarters of a mile in length, and a number of very long curves which are only slightly banked; when the course turns more abruptly, the banking is steeper, but never high enough to enable cars to travel around the turns at maximum speed.

Drivers competing at Monza soon discovered that the fastest way to cover the course was to drive as high as possible on the low bankings, which was both dangerous and difficult, and within a few years of the track's opening it became apparent that modern speeds had grown altogether too high for the course. Several fatal crashes occurred, the worst of which took place in 1928, during the European Grand Prix.

A car driven by Emilio Materassi, coming out of the south curve into the straight past the grandstands, left the track and crashed through the railings into the spectators. More than twenty people were killed, and twice as many were injured. Five years later Monza was the scene of another tragedy. Two of Italy's finest drivers—Campari and Borzacchini—both skidded on the south curve, as a result of oil spilt on the track; Borzacchini's machine overturned, and Campari's left the course and struck a tree. Both men were killed, while two more cars also crashed at the same spot shortly afterwards. A little later yet another driver—Czaykowski—lost control on this curve, his machine turning over and catching fire. He, too, was killed.

Following these disasters, the authorities built a new section to the track which made it possible to use only the inner portion of the course; this, by reason of its curves, reduced the speeds of competing cars. The restricted course, however, lessens the value of the circuit for racing, making it apparent that the Monza track can be restored to its former popularity only by considerable modification. The crack Italian drivers, indeed, often test out their cars on *Autostrada*—special motor roads—in preference to using Monza.

Until 1924 the countries possessing motor-racing tracks were England, America, Germany, and Italy. In this year France joined them with the completion of the Linas-Montlhèry autodrome, intended as the finest racing track in the world; the road circuit, over which the French Grand Prix is run, was added later.

This course is given an oval form by the inclusion of two short straights on opposite sides, otherwise the circuit would be a true bowl. The track is sixty feet wide, and the banking rises to a height of over thirty-four feet. The surface is easily the smoothest of any track; because of this, and of the fact that a car can maintain sustained speed all the way round, Montlhèry has become a centre for record breaking.

TRACK RACING

The track has been the setting for record attempts which range from a dash over one mile to others in which a car has travelled continuously for eight weeks, covering over eighty thousand miles. Brooklands' fastest car—the Napier-Railton—was taken there for an attempt upon the twenty-four hours' record. It was hoped to keep the car running for day and night at an average speed of 120 m.p.h., and for twenty hours this schedule was maintained. Then, at dawn, rain fell and the machine skidded off one banking. The driver held it all along the following straight, but the machine slid upwards when it reached the farther banking; one wheel went over the upper edge, then the car swung round and slid down the track again, diving off the course on to soft earth.

Hardly any races are held around the track itself, although part of it is employed when the road circuit is used. It is devoted almost entirely to record attempts, and 75 per cent of existing records have been broken there. The course carried out fully the intention of its designer—that it should be in the nature of a real laboratory for high-speed work.

In complete contrast is Germany's Nurburg Ring, the largest specially constructed motor-racing course in the world. It stands in the Eifel hills, about forty-five miles from Cologne, and the full circuit measures over seventeen miles. It required two years to construct, but can hardly be regarded as a true speed track, because it winds among the hills, with very sudden gradients, abrupt bends, and sharp curves. The course turns so much that every brief straight, every corner and each hill has been named as an aid to drivers in memorizing the circuit.

The course is so difficult that when the world's fastest road-racing cars competed in the German Grand Prix of 1934, the winner averaged only 75·1 m.p.h. The quality of the circuit may be gauged from this, and the relatively low speed helps to make clear why the Nurburg Ring is an enclosed motor course rather than a track; the point may be still further stressed by the fact that the car which won this Grand Prix was capable of a rate of travel in excess of 180 m.p.h.

There are but four more true motor-racing tracks. One is on the Littorio aerodrome, near Rome; this is formed by concrete runways built to facilitate the 'take-off' of heavy aeroplanes in bad weather. The runways, linked by banked curves, have created a short course. Another track exists at Sitges, in Barcelona; this has a lap distance of only one and a quarter miles, and is similar to the American board tracks, except that it is surfaced with concrete. Yet another course, with a lap distance of less than two miles, is in existence at San Martin, near Buenos Aires; this is an oval with a pair of one thousand yard straights.

The only other motor track is at Miramas, twenty-five miles north-west of Marseilles. This consists of a circle of concrete, about fifty feet wide and a little more than three miles in circumference. It has no banking, and it now stands quite desolate and disused. It has a magnificent grandstand and excellent equipment, but the course is too remote from the car manufacturing centres, and the track itself is not designed for present-day speeds.

It is beyond question that Brooklands has contributed more to motoring and motor racing than any track ever constructed. Every leading English race driver has used it to learn the not easy art of handling a fast car and, in

35 FIVE CARS BUNCHED IN A TURN ON THE MONZA TRACK DURING THE ITALIAN GRAND PRIX

36 AT THE NURBURG RING, GERMANY, THE WORLD'S BIGGEST ARTIFICIAL MOTOR RACING COURSE

the course of time, a great many of the Continental racing men have found occasion to visit the track.

In a degree that is altogether more specialized, the Linas-Montlhèry autodrome has contributed much, and it is plain that Indianapolis—by staging one outstanding event in the year—has sustained interest in motor racing in America. The plan of the Avus course and of the track at Monza lessens the ability of these circuits to contribute a great deal to motor racing, the potentialities of both being restricted by their design. Avus, however, as already mentioned, is attracting increasing attention as a centre for high-speed record attempts.

CHAPTER IV

ROUND-THE-HOUSES RACES

THE most interesting development in modern motor racing is undoubtedly the introduction of events run over short circuits planned within the confines of a town. These have become known as 'round-the-houses' races, the first of which was the Grand Prix of Monaco, inaugurated in 1929.

The attraction of such events lies in the spectacle of cars racing through the streets at speeds which, in the ordinary way, would be abnormal. The noise of the machines is stirringly echoed by the surrounding buildings and, of course, the whole life of the town is brought to a temporary standstill.

The daring of the idea behind such an event may be appreciated if a rough equivalent of the Monaco circuit were schemed through London streets. Such a course would start on the Embankment, turning past the Houses of Parliament into Whitehall, then around Trafalgar Square to the Strand, returning to the Embankment by way of the Adelphi Arches. Or, in New York, it would be necessary to contrive a course running down Broadway to Battery Park, doubling back through the streets behind the East Side docks.

Such imaginary circuits indicate the conditions under which a round-the-houses race is run, although neither would actually duplicate the course at Monaco, where the surroundings change from what is very beautiful to a section which is both drab and dangerous. Cars start on a road just behind the promenade at La Condamine—

37 A SECTION OF THE COURSE EMPLOYED FOR THE GRAND PRIX OF PAU

38 LUIGI FAGIOLI, WINNER OF THE GRAND PRIX DE MONACO, 1935, RUNNING DOWN THE PROMENADE ALONG THE SEA FRONT AT MONTE CARLO

39 THE STRAIN OF DRIVING IS SHOWN BY THE ATTITUDES OF THESE DRIVERS ON THE MONACO CIRCUIT, 1935. A MASERATI LEADS LORD HOWE'S BUGATTI THROUGH THE TURN

ROUND-THE-HOUSES RACES

adjacent to Monte Carlo—and at once race up a steep slope overlooked by tall buildings. From the crest of the rise, the road swings around the lovely gardens before the famous casino at Monte Carlo, then drops into a section filled with dangerous turns, finally diving beneath a railway arch out to the sea front. The course runs through a short tunnel under the *Tir aux Pigeons*, then curves gently for some five hundred yards before it suddenly sweeps on to the paving of the promenade, leaving the road altogether. The circuit follows this paving in order to make a hairpin near a gasworks, from which it returns to the starting-point.

The total lap distance is just two miles, and such straights as exist are very short, while the corners are not easy to take. The circuit is generally regarded by racing men as imposing a greater physical strain than any other in existence, because of the number of corners; during the race a car is taking turns at the average rate of one every twenty seconds. Men usually go into very strict training for weeks in advance of the event.

When the race was first run in 1929 it was open to anyone, but it soon became evident that the circuit demanded a very high degree of skill; for this reason only men invited by the organizers may now compete. As a result, the start sees an assembly of the most brilliant drivers on the Continent; despite this, the highest average speed ever set up for the race is only 58·1 m.p.h., achieved by Fagioli with a Mercédès-Benz in 1935.

All danger-points are guarded by sandbags or straw bales, while motor-boats patrol the harbour, ready to go to the assistance of any driver whose car might smash through the promenade parapet and fall into the sea. The circuit is such that it is impossible to arrange for escape roads on all the corners, with the result that the least error of judgment almost inevitably means a crash.

In the 1932 race Louis Chiron touched a sandbag on the corner where the road turns on to the actual promenade, just as he was passing two other machines. His car left the ground, tilting over and flinging him out; he fell in front of the other two machines which, however, avoided him, while his own car rammed the sandbags head on. Chiron was bruised and shaken and, although not badly hurt, he was the more unfortunate because, at that time, he held the lead.

Serious crashes during the race are rare, partly because the cars can nowhere attain really high speed, and partly because of the high standard of driving, but the event invariably has dramatic moments. In the 1933 race Tazio Nuvolari fought a tremendous duel against Varzi over the concluding laps. They went round with hardly the length of a car between them, covering some seventeen laps in this way until, on the last lap, Nuvolari broke an oil-pipe and coasted along the promenade while Varzi went ahead. Smoke poured from Nuvolari's cockpit, and he climbed from his seat, perching on the tail of his machine until the car stopped, then he got out and pushed it on to the finishing line, hoping at least to secure second place. He received assistance in pushing the machine, however, and was disqualified.

In the following year's race Louis Chiron took the lead from the start and by half distance he was three-quarters of a minute ahead, with Philippe Etancelin, René Dreyfus, and young Guy Moll pursuing him. Etancelin skidded by the casino ten laps later, slid into sandbags and damaged his car, so that he was obliged to retire, while Moll passed Dreyfus and so took second place. Chiron increased his lead until two laps from the end,

40 MACHINES RACING ALONG THE PROMENADE IN THE GRAND PRIX AUTOMOBILE DE NICE

41 IN THE MANNIN BEG RACE. 'FREDDIE' DIXON IS CORNERING WITH A RILEY

42 COUNT TROSSI TAKING HIS ALFA-ROMEO THROUGH A TURN IN THE GRAND PRIX DE VICHY, HELD OVER A $1\frac{1}{2}$ MILES COURSE ENTIRELY INSIDE THE TOWN

43 IN THE FIRST CIRCUITO DI BIELLA, 1934. COUNT FELICE TROSSI, WINNER OF THE RACE

44 CORNERING OVER TRAMLINES, CLOSE BY SANDBAGS PLACED TO GUARD A LETTERBOX JUTTING FROM THE WALL. ACHILLE VARZI, WITH AN ALFA-ROMEO, IN THE BIELLA RACE

45 THE FINISH OF THE MANNIN MOAR, 1935, A 'ROUND-THE-HOUSES' RACE AT DOUGLAS, ISLE OF MAN

ROUND-THE-HOUSES RACES

when he appeared certain to win, then he skidded on a turn by the railway station, ramming the sandbags. While he tried to extricate his machine, Moll flashed past him to win the race.

In 1935 the event was completely dominated by the Mercédès-Benz which Luigi Fagioli drove. He led the race from start to finish, at a pace which was largely responsible for the fact that only eight of the fifteen starters were on the course when he won, half of them being three or more laps behind.

The success of the Grand Prix de Monaco has resulted in the organization of similar events. At Pau, another town in the south of France, exists a circuit which is even more difficult than that at Monte Carlo. It is hardly one and a half miles in length, with considerably more corners and bends. The only level stretch lasts for barely three hundred yards; there is one other straight of equal length, but this runs up a gradient. The majority of the corners are unpleasant, and when the race was run in 1933 the winner was able to average only 43·3 m.p.h. Incidentally, this event was held during February, when Pau was snowbound; the race started in a snowstorm, making matters very difficult for the drivers.

An altogether more effective round-the-houses circuit is that for the Mannin Beg and Mannin Moar races at Douglas, Isle of Man, the former event being for cars of under 1,500 c.c. and the latter for machines of unlimited capacity. The series began in 1933, over a course which ran along the promenade then turned into the town, the back of the circuit incorporating a series of difficult corners; the route was altered for 1934, these turns being eliminated while the length was reduced from 4·6 to 3·7 miles.

When the races were first held the inhabitants of Douglas discovered that their freedom was considerably curtailed. Streets had to be closed, so that almost all business in the town was brought to a halt. As the event took place during the holiday season there was some complaint from visitors, with the result that, for 1934, the races were held some five or six weeks earlier in the year, when they proved a real success.

The Mannin Beg was marked by considerable excitement; at the end of the first lap the leading car hit sandbags placed to guard a refuge on a corner at the end of the promenade. The race settled down into a close fight between half a dozen machines, and ended in a victory for an M.G. Magnette, with four more cars of the same make following the winner home.

The driving in this race was altogether different from that at Monaco. The machines were smaller, but they were handled with a zest which was duplicated when the Mannin Moar—for cars of unlimited capacity—was held two days later. It was won by an Alfa-Romeo at a speed of 75·3 m.p.h., against which the average of 70·9 m.p.h., set up by the smaller cars in the race, compares very favourably.

In the round-the-houses race, high maximum speed does not necessarily bring a car home in front of the rest. At Monaco it is possible to use top gear only for two brief periods around the circuit, and even on the longer Douglas course there are very few stretches where a car can be worked up to within reach of its highest speed.

The most pleasant of all town circuits is that at Nice, where the course is very simple and quite flat. The cars start down one side of the Promenade des Anglais,

46 DURING THE 'ROUND-THE-HOUSES' RACE AT MONTREUX. WHITNEY STRAIGHT'S MASERATI CLEARING A CORNER

47 THE OPEL ROCKET CAR. AFTER ACHIEVING HIGH SPEEDS, AN ACCIDENT RESULTED IN THE COMPLETE ANNIHILATION OF THE MACHINE

48 A FRENCH ENGINEER DESIGNED THIS CAR FOR ATTEMPTS ON WORLD'S RECORDS. IT WAS EVENTUALLY BURNT OUT DURING TESTS ON THE SANDS AT LA BAULE

running past islands from which palm-trees grow, with small fountains playing between them. Where the promenade narrows, the cars make a hairpin turn, coming back along the promenade until they reach the Jardin du Roi Albert Premier. They run around this, returning to the promenade and completing the lap. The course measures exactly two miles, fringed almost all the way by palm-trees and flower-beds.

Since the circuit is an easy one, it gives opportunity for very keen work on the part of drivers, while the crowd which gathers behind the bales of straw lining the course is always very large, the roofs and balconies, entrances and windows of big hotels along the promenade being used to accommodate thousands more spectators. As the circuit is so short, cars are constantly passing any given point, holding the interest of the crowd and maintaining an excitement which, by the time the race ends, has usually become too much for the watchers. In the last two races the crowd swarmed on to the course as soon as the winner crossed the line; in 1934 Varzi won at a speed of 65·7 m.p.h., and the invasion of the spectators then brought the race to an end, so that the cars behind his were unable actually to complete the course.

In round-the-houses events, braking power and acceleration are vital features, while the machines run so much in their intermediate gears that the cockpits become exceedingly hot. In the 1934 Nice race, one driver was forced to retire because the heat from his gear-box burned his legs; Varzi suffered from the same trouble, although he was able to keep his car in the lead.

Protection for spectators is vitally necessary; seven thousand straw bales are employed at Nice, placed in a barrier around the circuit as a guard against any errors of judgment which might be made by drivers in the excitement of the race. Cars have hit the bales on many occasions, always with such force that, without their protection, grave accidents must have followed, since spectators were everywhere standing ten feet deep behind the barriers.

There is one other similar circuit in France, and this is at Nîmes, where cars run on either side of a broad boulevard, with hazards formed by artificial turns, but the event is not one of particular importance.

The first round-the-houses race in Italy was staged in October 1934 at Biella. This was held over a course very little more than one and a quarter miles in length; the circuit proved so difficult that only seven cars were allowed to start at a time, and as there were twenty-seven entrants, the race had to be run off in heats, the final being won at 52·5 m.p.h. The course contains one short steep hill, a hairpin turn, and several very abrupt corners. The Biella race was followed by another round-the-houses event at Modena over a similar circuit. Both events were run off amidst very great excitement, the Italians welcoming what was, to them, a novelty in motor sport.

It is impossible to judge to what extent such races will continue to hold a place in the international calendar. Their great defect is that they temporarily disrupt the normal habits of townsfolk, but compensation lies in the fact that a round-the-houses event is unequalled for excitement and colour.

Probably they will continue, because no other type of race has yet been contrived which imposes so great a strain on the gear-box and transmission of a car, or puts such a premium upon acceleration.

A peculiar aspect of round-the-houses work is that

although it looks very dangerous, it is not quite so hazardous as it appears, because the number of corners makes the speed of machines relatively low. At the same time such courses, in making their definite demand for driving skill, serve to increase the ability of the men who take part in them.

Of existing circuits, the one at Monaco is easily the best, and contributes most to motor racing. The Grand Prix which is held there has grown from an experiment to one of the most important of all races. This alone suggests that round-the-houses events will be held for many years to come, and it is not unlikely that their numbers will still further increase.

CHAPTER V

PIT-WORK

IN the earliest long-distance races, drivers soon discovered that it was necessary to make arrangements for fresh supplies of petrol, oil, and water, for new tyres and for the replacement of parts which might have become damaged or broken. At first they carried all tools, spare parts, and tyres on their machines, relying upon being able to replenish their petrol tanks at the towns through which they passed.

When cars began to run over closed circuits, the drivers found that it was not necessary to carry so much on their cars because, if depots were established at the side of the course, they were able to pull up and secure anything that might be required. In this way replenishment depots—or 'pits'—came into existence, the operating of which has now become an art in itself.

In modern races these pits are set in a long line, usually opposite the grandstand; the work carried out at a pit can materially affect the result of a race, and is always of considerable interest to onlookers. The pits usually resemble small sheds, generally roofed in and separated from those on either side by wire mesh; the front is quite open and has a counter set at about waist height, on which are placed such tools as may be required.

The immediate function of a replenishment pit is to service the car and assist the driver. It is stocked with supplies of fuel and oil and spare parts, a first-aid chest, refreshments for the driver, quick-lift jacks, spare wheels and tyres—in fact, everything which ingenuity can contrive

49 AN AUTO-UNION HALTED AT ITS PIT DURING PRACTICE ON THE AVUS TRACK

50 PREPARATIONS BEFORE THE START. THE TRACK WAS WET, AND THE TYRES HAVE BEEN SPECIALLY TREATED WITH SHALLOW CUTS TRAVERSING THE NORMAL TREAD

and imagination can suggest as being likely to prove useful during the race. In addition, it is the function of those in charge to inform the driver of his position and, generally, to control his driving by means of signals.

These pit signals are of vital importance, because a man has little means of judging his position in a race after the first ten or fifteen laps. In a scratch race he knows where he is, but when involved handicapping is employed—such as exists in Great Britain—the driver needs to be told almost from the outset the place in which he is running. He rarely has an opportunity of reading the lap scoreboard as he goes by, although even if he could this would not help him very much. The men in the pit are able to see exactly the position of their own car and of all others; by timing rival machines they can judge whether to signal their driver to travel faster, or to slow down and spare his engine.

That a driver should ever slow down during an event is at variance with the opinion held by many unversed in the tactics of motor racing. It is quite often thought that a driver simply puts his foot down on the throttle pedal and travels, from start to finish, just as hard as he can make his car move. This is quite wrong, and it is a fact that a good driver goes only as fast as is necessary to fend off a rival's attack. Even if he is behind the leader, he does not drive flat out, but only fast enough to enable him to overtake and pass before the end of the race.

It is necessary to make this important point quite clear if one vital function of pit-work is to be fully understood. If a driver were one lap—representing, say, five miles—behind the leader in a race with thirty laps still to be covered, the driver would not try to regain that lap in one desperate burst of speed. Instead, he would try to make up the quarter of a mile on each of twenty laps, so that when the race had only ten laps to cover, he would be in a position to challenge the leader and to pass him. At the same time, there would remain a safety margin of ten laps in case the leader should increase his pace.

It is quite impossible for a driver to work out for himself just how fast he would have to go in order to accomplish this; should the car ahead increase its speed, he would have no means of learning it, if the matter were left to himself. It is here that his pit assists him. Those who man the depot would give him signals, telling him precisely how much faster to go on any given lap; it is they who would work out his position and that of the car he had to challenge, timing them both and so arranging matters that their own machine countered every effort made by its rival.

The speed of cars is, thus, actually controlled far more by the pits than by the men who drive, and for this reason every driver glances at his pit each time he passes, and should obey such orders as may be given him from it.

In the ordinary way, pit signals are simple, consisting of 'Faster,' 'Slower,' 'O.K.' or 'Come In.' At one time they were usually conveyed by different symbols: signs placed at the end of a short, slender pole; the order to go faster might be given by a red triangle, and 'O.K.' might be indicated by a green square, and so on. The normal practice now is to use a painted board, to the centre of which a pointer has been attached; the indicator gives an order in accordance with the position in which it is set.

Present-day speeds are so high that the difference between machines fighting out a race usually amounts only to a matter of seconds, and the timing of the cars is specialized work, demanding great accuracy. The whole matter becomes very complicated when a pit is controlling a team of three cars. It grows as involved as movements on a chessboard, and computations have to be made so swiftly that, more than once, the assistance of accountants has been secured to support the work of the men with stop-watches.

Each pit is, of course, careful to do everything possible to prevent the men in other depots learning the meaning of their signals. For important events, drivers and teams often change their pit signals from race to race, although every effort is made to keep them as simple as possible. Frequently a control station is set up in some place other than the pits, communication between pit and station being maintained by messengers or even by field telephone. In such circumstances, signals become comparatively secret, and the station is always set up at the side of a long straight, so that a driver has plenty of time to see what order is being given him and, equally important, to acknowledge the instruction.

In addition to signals, a driver may be shown a board which will indicate his position in a race, and his speed. Sometimes he will be given the number of the car ahead, and the time lapse between the two cars. In that case a board bearing 12/19 would indicate that the driver was nineteen seconds behind car No. 12, and he would then drive until he overtook it. This method is the one often adopted by independent drivers, usually near the close of a race, when there is everything to be gained by driving hard in order to win or to be placed, and very little to lose.

Good work with pit signals, and efficient time-keeping, are nullified unless every precaution is taken to ensure that when a car does stop for attention it is sent into the race again with the least possible delay. For this reason a pit must be thoroughly organized, with preparations made for every emergency, while driver and mechanics must be practised in such movements as may be required—whether for replenishment or in effecting a minor adjustment—to get the car off once more.

The equipment of a well-organized pit consists, first, of the tools set out along the counter, each being in an appointed place which has been memorized by the driver and the mechanics who will work on the car when it comes in. Heavy equipment is usually placed beneath the counter itself, while spare wheels and tins of petrol and oil are at the back of the pit. The timekeepers are given one end of the counter at which to work, and near them stand the pit signals which are being used in the race.

Invariably, one man has complete control of the pit; his responsibility is to see that everything works smoothly, that all is ready for an emergency, and that preparations are made to receive the car when it stops for replenishment according to schedule.

In a modern Grand Prix a driver expects to call at his pit but once. He usually starts with sufficient petrol to carry him well over half-distance and, the car's petrol consumption being known, he is told before he starts on what lap he must make his pit stop; he does not, however, come in until he receives a signal to do so, taking this at the start of the lap prior to his halt.

While that signal is being flown for him, final preparations are made in the pit. Mechanics, watching the car as it passes on earlier laps, determine whether wheel changes are necessary; in all probability the rear tyres will have been worn down, so spare wheels are made

51 PIT SIGNALS: AN IMPORTANT FUNCTION OF ANY DEPOT

52 SIX MEN AT WORK ON A CAR WHICH CHECKED AT ITS PIT DURING THE TWENTY-FOUR-HOURS BOL D'OR RACE, HELD NEAR PARIS

53 AN AUTO-UNION AT THE REPLENISHMENT PITS

PIT-WORK

ready. Five-gallon metal churns are filled with filtered fuel, and are set—with a filler funnel—at one end of the counter, while spouted cans containing oil and water are placed opposite the point where the front of the car will be when the machine halts.

A glass containing some liquid refreshment—lemonade or champagne—is prepared for the driver, together with a couple of sandwiches; sometimes a first-aid box is put against these, in case his face should have been cut by flying stones. The mechanics who are to aid with the car perch themselves on the pit counter, ready to jump down to the course, the pit manager takes up a position where he can watch everything, the remainder of the staff stand by ready to obey orders so that, when the car comes into sight, slowing for its stop, everything is absolutely ready.

The instant that the car halts, each man leaps to his appointed task. In all probability it is the driver's work to attend to water and oil, while the mechanics replenish the petrol tank and change the rear wheels. Whatever the arrangement may be, it is certain that every move has been practised thoroughly and completely, with the result that the driver is back in the cockpit just as the mechanics' work is completed, when the car goes off again.

In some cases the driver may not leave his cockpit at all, remaining in his seat while mechanics attend to the machine; this depends largely upon the regulations covering pit-work, and the schedule planned for the stop. Most drivers prefer to remain in the car, glad of a short rest.

It is natural that everything about a car should have been arranged to facilitate fast pit-work. Every racing machine has quick-release filler caps for radiator and petrol tank, which can be fully opened at a single blow from the hand. The funnels used to convey petrol to the tank can accommodate five gallons of fluid without overflowing; the man carrying out this work has only to lift each churn in turn from the counter, spill its contents into the funnel, pitch the churn back, and reach for another until all have been emptied. Usually, four or five are required.

The jacks employed to raise an axle are a quick-lift type, which elevate the wheels in a single movement; all wheels have knock-off hub-caps, so that a wheel may be removed and another set in its place in an incredibly short space of time. As an indication of how fast pit-work can be, it was in the French Grand Prix of 1934 that Louis Chiron made two pit stops; at the first all four wheels were changed, while the machine was replenished with water and petrol in exactly 100 seconds. Later in the race he stopped again, this time to refuel and change his rear wheels in 55 seconds.

A halt for adjustments or repairs greatly reduces a car's chances in a race. This may be realized from the results of some of the more important races in the 1934 season. At Indianapolis the winner finished only 28 seconds in front of the car which ran into second place; this was at the end of a race over a distance of five hundred miles, and the difference in time between the two cars shows how little margin exists for pit-work of any sort. At Monaco the winner was only 62 seconds in the lead, and in the French Grand Prix Chiron finished just three minutes ahead of the second car; much of that three minutes had been gained as a result of his fast replenishment work. Varzi, who took second place, spent 1 minute 10 seconds longer at his pit than Chiron

54 AT THE PITS DURING THE GRAN PREMIO D'ITALIA ON MONZA TRACK. THE CAR IS NUVOLARI'S MASERATI

55 CONCENTRATED PIT-WORK ON ACHILLE VARZI'S CAR DURING THE ITALIAN GRAND PRIX, 1934, WHEN HE HELD SECOND PLACE IN THE RACE

56 FREDDIE DIXON'S CAR AT THE PITS IN THE B.R.D.C. 500 MILES RACE, 1934

during the event, although on each occasion both cars were given precisely the same attention.

The closeness of these times suggests that a driver whose car requires much attention during an important event can have little hope of victory. On the other hand, there exists in motor racing a point of honour that a driver should, if at all possible, keep his car going, making repairs that will send the machine out again, even though the delays make it impossible to gain a place in the race, or even to finish the set distance.

At one time pit-work during the Indianapolis races was usually regarded as the best in the world, while German mechanics and drivers always appeared especially well-drilled and efficient. Nowadays, however, there is very little to choose between the different nationalities, although some of the Italian teams in the Grand Prix races have very effective pit organization.

The whole matter is largely one of careful preparation and much practice, and differs with the character of each race. In very fast, close events the work must be extremely rapid, but in endurance and very long-distance races thoroughness is more important than the loss of a few seconds. It is, in any case, a vital detail, where inefficiency can ruin the chances of a driver and a car just as effectively as the failure of some part of the machine itself.

CHAPTER VI

RECORD BREAKING

It was in 1922 that really high speed was first obtained from a car specially built to break records. An American driver—Sig. Haugdahl—achieved a speed of 180·27 m.p.h. over a distance of one mile at Daytona Beach, Florida, gaining the distinction of being the first man actually to reach three miles a minute.

He used a car which he himself had designed, fitted with a 250 h.p. engine, the machine being very carefully streamlined. During his first trials, Haugdahl found that when he reached a speed of 150 m.p.h. the car became subject to tremendous vibration. He altered the gear ratios and reached 160 m.p.h., when the vibration returned and made it impossible to travel faster. He ascertained that the shaking was not caused by the engine, and came to the conclusion that the trouble lay with his tyres.

As a test, he fitted each of his wheels on to a dummy hub, and discovered that a heavy spot on each tyre always brought the spinning wheel to rest in the same position; by placing lead at the opposite side he was able to balance the wheel. When this had been done to each wheel, he took his car out again, and this time reached three miles a minute. He found driving at that speed very dangerous, because it was hard to keep the car in a straight line, and in those days steering gears had not reached their present state of perfection.

Haugdahl's effort was not accepted as a world's record. In order to register such a record it is necessary to make

57 WHITNEY STRAIGHT ATTACKING THE BROOKLANDS LAP RECORD WITH A DUESENBERG

REPLENISHMENT AND WHEEL-CHANGING DURING A STOP WHILE THIS HOTCHKISS CAR WAS ATTACKING RECORDS AT MONTLHÈRY

two runs over the measured mile, one in either direction, the average speed of the two efforts counting for the record. The reason for this regulation is that if the wind or the course assists a car on one run, those conditions are against it on the return trip.

The importance of this American attempt lies in the things that were learned from it. Haugdahl increased his possible speed from 160 m.p.h. not by enhanced engine power or by better streamlining, but simply by balancing his wheels and tyres; this has now come to be normal practice with all cars, whether they race or make record attempts.

This discovery that wheels require to be balanced serves to indicate the value of record breaking. The whole object of such efforts is to show the superior speed of a particular car; if it can attain a greater rate of travel than others of its type, it is obvious that it must be more efficient. It must, in other words, have features which are an improvement upon those of the cars which have made earlier attempts; those features, passed on to racing machines and, in turn, to ordinary cars, do much to improve motoring in general.

It would be unwise to suggest that Sig. Haugdahl was the first man to discover the need to balance wheels. Other men, making similar attempts, also discovered the need, proving what he had found, and in this way record attempts serve to check and re-check such details.

It is necessary to appreciate that every effort to raise a record means that the driver must do a little more than anyone has done before, whether he is attacking a class record with a small car, or whether he is attempting to raise the world's land-speed. This applies particularly to efforts over short distances, from the mile to ten miles, where the car has to be brought to the greatest pitch of efficiency, because success depends upon gaining only fractions of a second.

In consequence, record breaking can be somewhat grim, as is shown by the land-speed attempts at Daytona. Wide interest in these efforts was created when the late Sir Henry Segrave reached 203 m.p.h. in 1927. Until he actually achieved this, there were many who believed that such pace was impossible, and that the suction caused by the car would tear up the course behind it. Segrave's success created so great a sensation that other cars were built to attack his record, and the following year Frank Lockhart crashed disastrously with his 'Black Hawk' Stutz.

During early trials, this beautifully designed machine got out of hand and ran into the sea. When repairs had been effected, Lockhart tried again, but a rear tyre deflated while he was moving at 200 m.p.h. The car skidded for five hundred feet, then covered a similar distance in a series of gigantic leaps, smashing itself against the sand before it came to a stop, Lockhart being flung out and killed.

There was another fatal accident the following year with 'Triplex,' a car which had held the record. It was being driven by Lee Bible when it got out of hand, leaving the marked course and killing a cinematograph operator who was photographing the attempt. The machine somersaulted half a dozen times before it came to rest against the sand-dunes, completely wrecked.

The reason for the crash was generally attributed to the fact that the driver must have closed the throttle too suddenly after clearing the measured mile. The enormous braking effect which resulted sent the car out of control.

63 SIR MALCOLM CAMPBELL COMING INTO THE MEASURED MILE AT DAYTONA BEACH. THE CAR WAS ON ITS NORTHWARD RUN AND IS SHOWN MOVING AT OVER 280 M.P.H.

64 'BLUE BIRD' BEING MADE FINALLY READY FOR WORLD'S RECORD ATTEMPTS AT DAYTONA BEACH, 1935

65 SIR MALCOLM CAMPBELL'S 'BLUE BIRD', THE WORLD'S FASTEST CAR. SPECIAL VANES, SEEN RAISED BEHIND THE REAR WHEELS, ACT AS WIND-BRAKES

66 ON THE AVUS TRACK, BERLIN. RUDOLF CARACCIOLA DURING A RECORD-BREAKING RUN WITH A MERCÉDÈS-BENZ

RECORD BREAKING

All the way down through the list of records efforts are marked by unfortunate mishaps, but the same can be said of any sphere of activity in which men endeavour to accomplish something better than anything which has already been done. And success does bring many benefits.

Ten years ago the highest speed ever attained by a 750 c.c. car was 84·2 m.p.h. The record for this size of car is now held with a speed of 130·8 m.p.h., more than half as fast again. The figure for larger machines is similar; ten years back no car of a capacity up to 5,000 c.c. had broken a record at more than 119 m.p.h.; the present record is held at around 200 m.p.h.

Although short-distance records have their value, they are hardly more than sprints in which a machine is lifted to a very high speed for only a short time. The pace achieved in the present land-speed record is a great feat from the technical standpoint, and is one of considerable national importance. Any effort to raise the world's land-speed record now requires much experience, and a tremendous complexity of organization. Sir Malcolm Campbell has shown, by his consistently successful attacks on this record, a great tenacity of purpose, and has proved the soundness of this country's engineering technique and ability.

It is the opinion of most racing men, however, that the world's hour record is, in some respects, of even greater interest, and is the most difficult of all to secure.

In this attempt a driver does not try simply to reach a particular rate of travel; instead, he endeavours to cover as many miles as possible in sixty minutes. Expressed differently, he does not attempt merely to do 120 m.p.h. over a short distance, but tries actually to cover one hundred and twenty miles in the hour, which is a very different thing.

The hour record is actually set at a much higher speed than this. In July 1935 it was raised to 152·7 m.p.h. by John Cobb, with his Napier-Railton. He made his effort on the Bonneville Salt Flats, in Utah, when he also succeeded in raising the world's twenty-four hours' record from 127·2 m.p.h. to 134·7 m.p.h., covering a distance of 3,235 miles.

In ten years the world's hour record has been lifted by only 30 m.p.h., but there is a very good reason for this. The driver requires to be at the peak of physical fitness, because the strain of driving for a full hour at absolute maximum speed is very great indeed. He cannot relax for one moment, and his driving must be completely faultless.

When John Cobb broke the record his attempt involved travelling over each of the 152 miles just about three seconds faster than had been achieved by the car which had set up the existing figures. That narrow margin helps to indicate the extreme pitch of keenness required in the hour attempt, and just as important is the condition of the car. There is no room for the least failure of mechanism, and any fault will spoil the effort; the car must be perfect.

It is because so much is demanded from driver and machine that the speed for the hour record has increased so slowly in the course of the last ten years. It is almost certain that the pace will be pushed higher, although it is very probable that it will rise but little, each successful effort lifting it by only a few miles per hour.

World's records range from that for the kilometre, taken from a standing start, up through short distances

67 THE 'SILVER BULLET' WAS UNSUCCESSFUL IN RECORD ATTEMPTS AT DAYTONA, BUT THE MACHINE IS REGARDED AS HAVING ALMOST PERFECT STREAMLINING

68 HANS VILLIEZ VON STUCK

69 WITH THIS SPECIALLY STREAMLINED AUTO-UNION, HANS VON STUCK ACHIEVED 199 M.P.H. ON AN ITALIAN AUTOSTRADA

70 A FRONTAL VIEW OF THE CAR WITH VON STUCK IN THE COMPLETELY ENCLOSED COCKPIT

71 THE *BIMOTORE* ALFA-ROMEO, A ROAD-RACING MACHINE WHICH HAS COVERED THE MEASURED MILE AT 200·8 M.P.H.

to the hour record, then on to the record for twenty-four hours, and others for distances which are very great. The longest world's record stands at 180,000 miles, made by a Citroën car at Montlhèry at an average speed of very little below 60 m.p.h. These world's records are for the fastest times set up over specific distances, or during particular periods of time, by cars irrespective of their engine size.

In addition, there exist what are known as International Class records. These start from Class A, for cars of over 8,000 c.c., and run down to Class J, which is for cars with engines of only 350 c.c.—that is, about the size of the average motor-cycle engine. All these records cover the same distance and time-range as world's records.

The great majority of records have been set up on the Linas-Montlhèry speedway and Brooklands, but some have been made in quite unusual places. Records have been taken on a stretch of road near Tat, in Hungary; others have been made on the bed of a dry lake at Muroc, U.S.A., and John Cobb's particularly fine series of long-distance figures was achieved on the bed of a dry salt lake in Utah.

These salt-beds are actually formed by a lake which dries up during the summer, leaving a deposit which is extremely hard. Cobb set out to attack all world's long-distance records, and was successful in gaining those between distances of one hundred and three thousand miles at speeds of above 130 m.p.h. A circle ten miles in circumference was marked out for him, and the car was driven around this continuously for twenty-four hours.

He used the salt-beds because there was no other site available, and certainly no artificial track exists which would have enabled him to reach such high continuous speed. His finest feat was, however, in setting up the new hour record, and the course itself was a great advantage to the driver.

It is often the case that a natural course is much more effective than one artificially constructed, although such an attempt involves considerable preparation and expense. Almost always these courses are not very accessible; the salt-beds are over a hundred and twenty miles from Salt Lake City, but have the advantage of being served by a railway line. Even then, timing officials and their equipment, the car and all its spare parts, fuel and wheels and mechanics have to be conveyed over great distances. Sir Malcolm Campbell once went out to a dry lake-bed in South Africa, travelling seventeen days to reach Cape Town, and then four hundred miles inland, accompanied by his car, some twenty crates of spare parts, his mechanics and timing officials.

Even when a site is conveniently placed, as at Daytona Beach, the work of marking out the course and making everything ready is very great. Every record attempt involves far more than the preparation of a car simply for a race; it is always preceded by weeks of work on the machine itself, whether the attempt is to last for only a few seconds or for twenty-four hours. Except in the case of land-speed record efforts at Daytona, the attempts are usually witnessed only by a handful of people technically interested.

Because of the remoteness of the Utah Salt beds, there were not very many spectators to watch Campbell when he achieved his ambition to surpass 300 m.p.h., a feat which he performed in early September, 1935. After a preliminary test, in which 'Blue Bird' reached about

72 BONNEVILLE SALT-BEDS, UTAH, ON WHICH SIR MALCOLM CAMPBELL ACHIEVED A SPEED OF OVER 304 M.P.H., AND WHERE MANY WORLD'S LONG-DISTANCE RECORDS HAVE BEEN BROKEN

73 'SPEED OF THE WIND,' A SPECIALLY BUILT CAR WITH WHICH CAPTAIN G. E. T. EYSTON HAS SET UP MANY NEW WORLD'S RECORDS ON BONNEVILLE SALT FLATS, UTAH

RECORD BREAKING

240 m.p.h., Campbell took his car out again on the following afternoon and, on his first run, covered the flying mile in 11·83 secs., which is equivalent to 304·3 m.p.h. On his return run he went through the mile at 12·08 secs., which gave him 298·01 m.p.h. The mean time of the two runs, and which establishes the record, was 11·95 secs., representing 301·12 m.p.h.

As the record which he had set up at Daytona, earlier in the year, stood at 276·8 m.p.h., Campbell had actually raised the world's land-speed by 25 m.p.h. In July, 1925, he had been the first man officially to drive a car at 150 m.p.h.; thus, it was almost exactly ten years later that he crowned his career by attaining just double the speed with which he had first introduced himself to the field of record breaking.

This fact in itself suggests how valuable is record breaking, because the land-speed record could not have been doubled in ten years but for the concentrated effort demanded by the work. In all record efforts, particularly those over short distances, there is no room for anything spectacular, although matters can be exciting enough for the driver, whatever the size of car he may be handling. From the moment of the start until he slows down he works at a very high pitch, travelling with the throttle pedal rammed absolutely flat, straining to secure the last fraction of power from his engine, because there can be no question of sparing a car for record work except in very long-distance attempts, when the machine must be handled with as wide a margin of safety as possible.

CHAPTER VII

HILL CLIMBING

THIS aspect of motor racing has an atmosphere of its own, and seems to demand distinct attributes in a driver. There are not many men who excel in hill-climb events, and who do equally well in road and track races.

The setting for a hill climb consists of a selected gradient, which usually incorporates a number of bends and corners. The courses are varied, and the only really important event held in England is at Shelsley Walsh hill, near Martley village, in Worcestershire; this course is just one thousand yards long and contains only two right-angle corners. At Freiburg, the setting for the annual German hill-climb Grand Prix, the course is seven and a half miles long and includes more than a hundred and fifty corners. The classic Mont Ventoux course, in France, is thirteen and a half miles in length and contains so many hairpin turns that they seem innumerable to competing drivers.

In these events a man races against time and runs without the handicap of other machines being on the road. In other words, the driver who takes his car from the starting-point to the finish in the shortest time is the winner of the climb. Because of this, the shorter the climb the greater the demand for driving ability; when a climb can be made in seconds only, the loss of even a fraction of time can rob a man of success.

This aspect of hill climbing is particularly well demonstrated at Shelsley Walsh, and some details of the course

74 A VIEW OF THE COURSE FOR THE HILL CLIMB UP THE STELVIO PASS

75 A BRITISH BUILT E.R.A. SETTING UP A NEW RECORD DURING THE SHELSLEY WALSH HILL CLIMB IN MAY, 1935

may make clearer the difficulties that it presents. Cars start on a gradient of one in eleven—that is, the road rises one foot for every eleven feet of its length. At the end of eighty yards is a distinct bend, after which the road straightens; the gradient increases steadily until, five hundred yards from the start, the slope has stiffened to one in six. At this point is a sharp left-hand corner, immediately followed by an equally abrupt right-hand turn; the road then continues in a straight climb to the finish.

In negotiating this hill a machine has to start in bottom gear, the driver making such gear changes as may be necessary to cover the ground to the first true corner at the highest possible speed. He has then to place his car in such a position that he can go through this turn without loss of time, and come out of it ready to take the next corner. In the case of a very fast machine the driver must ease his speed if he is to clear the first turn, otherwise he will skid and lose time. Some drivers, when going into this corner at Shelsley, actually employ the hand-brake and, at the same time, use the throttle to the full. On a very light car, specially built for such hill-climb work, employing the hand-brake does help to steady the machine; the fact that the car is accelerating would appear to produce an anomalous situation, but the plan works out in practice, and helps to show that it is sometimes profitable to handle a car in an unorthodox manner on a hill.

If a driver comes out of the first turn badly placed for the next corner, he will be slowed by the necessity for bringing his machine into position, while, of course, a skid only makes matters worse. Once through the second turn, the rest of the course is simply a straight dash to the finish, but a high degree of skill and precision is demanded in clearing the twin corners and reaching the straight at all quickly.

Just how difficult is hill climbing may be judged from the fact that it required ten years to lower the Shelsley record by ten seconds. In 1924 the record for the hill stood at 50·5 secs., and in June 1934 Whitney Straight climbed the hill in exactly 40 secs., after the figure had been gradually lowered during the intervening years. Straight used a supercharged Maserati, fitted with twin rear wheels to reduce wheel-spin and give him greater acceleration. In 1935 the record was brought still lower by Raymond Mays, who employed a 2-litre E.R.A., also with twin rear wheels; he set the figure at two-fifths of a second lower than Straight's time, bringing it down to $39\frac{3}{5}$ secs.

His car had less engine power than the Maserati, and it is a fact that great horsepower is not necessary on a hill of this type. Really terrific acceleration is a first essential, and after this it is the personal skill and determination of the driver which counts. The Shelsley Walsh hill climb is a most popular event and always draws great crowds, because the spectacle of a well-driven car, roaring up the steep gradient between the trees, is as attractive as it is thrilling.

The Shelsley course is one of the shortest of all hill climbs, and the majority of those held on the Continent are altogether longer. An outstanding event is that on the Stelvio Pass; in a distance of 8·6 miles over this remarkable mountain road, cars have to clear no less than forty-eight hairpin turns, and the finish is set nine thousand feet above sea-level.

This sinuous course was covered in 15 mins. 1·4 secs. by Mario Tadini in 1934—he drove an Alfa-Romeo—

and this is equivalent to a speed of 55·9 m.p.h. In comparison, the speed of Raymond Mays' run at Shelsley is only about 51·5 m.p.h., but the English course is so much shorter that the car has no chance anywhere to attain maximum speed; also, the two turns are very abrupt and difficult, while all the hairpins on the Stelvio are properly engineered and banked.

The quality of driving necessary for success in any hill climb is the same, whether the course be long or short. This is proved by the fact that Whitney Straight set up a new record at Mont Ventoux, prior to his fine run at Shelsley in 1934. This French course is fairly easy for the first four miles, after which bends and corners rapidly become more and more difficult, the final five miles consisting of one hairpin turn after another. Straight handled his car in much the same way here as at Shelsley—climbing steadily and taking the turns cleanly.

Possibly the most important climb in Europe, however, is that over the Klausen Pass, in Switzerland. This course is even more formidable than the one over the Stelvio, while it is only a matter of yards shorter than that for Mont Ventoux. It has more than one hundred bends and corners, in addition to a score of hairpin turns. Very bad weather preceded the 1934 event, and a landslide near the mountain village of Umerboden threatened to block the road, while rain and wind had so loosened boulders on the steep slopes beside the course that minor avalanches fell during the climb, fortunately without mishap.

It was the finest meeting ever held on the hill, and every important Continental racing stable was represented. The course is such that it is impossible for any driver to become familiar with it, so that the event resolves itself into an individual test of skill. Before the climb the record stood at 15 mins. 50 secs., and this time had been set up in 1932 by Rudolf Caracciola, with an Alfa-Romeo. He was now driving a new Mercédès-Benz, and his chief rival was Hans von Stuck, who was handling an Auto-Union.

The course was very wet, and was rendered dangerous in some places by patches of drifting mist, adding to the difficulty of handling Grand Prix type racing machines. Despite the state of the road, and the general conditions, von Stuck broke the record with a climb in 15 mins. 25 secs., but he made one error during his drive. He skidded on a turn, his car travelling broadside before he could straighten it. Caracciola, however, made an absolutely faultless climb on his Mercédès, registering 15 mins. 22·2 secs., beating von Stuck's time and establishing a new record.

The average speed achieved by Caracciola was just a little above 52 m.p.h., which appears low. The physical strain, however, of handling a racing car on the Klausen Pass is not light, and fifteen minutes of the constant and unremitting attention necessary takes a great toll.

A gradient known as Pike's Peak forms the only important hill climb in America. The course here is some twelve miles in length, formed by a succession of hairpin turns, between which the road climbs steeply. The record stands at 16 mins. 1·125 secs., but the climb has never been attempted by European racing cars; most of the American drivers who attack the hill use track-racing machines.

American drivers show little interest in hill climbs, so that the sport is confined almost entirely to Europe where, it must be admitted, it has been brought to an art. It is now rare for records to be lowered by more than a few

76 AT MONT VENTOUX. WHITNEY STRAIGHT TAKING HIS MASERATI THROUGH A BANKED TURN

77 DUST FLYING IN THE MULDERS' DRIFT HILL CLIMB CHAMPIONSHIP, SOUTH AFRICA. THIS MACHINE SET UP A NEW RECORD

78 A BEND ON THE COURSE FOR THE MONT VENTOUX HILL CLIMB

HILL CLIMBING

seconds even on long hills. Where the course is very short, fractions of a second count, and it is here that hill climbing produces definite risks.

In an endeavour to gain split seconds, a driver has to handle his car as closely as he dare to the limit of safety and, upon occasion, this necessity has brought disaster —instanced by the Chateau-Thierry hill climb, when this was held in May 1935. This is a classic climb, the course being one kilometre in length, and is one of the oldest of French events, but the regulations governing it are a little unusual. Drivers have to bring their cars to a stop at the end of the kilometre, which results in very fierce braking as the finish of the climb is reached.

In the past there had been accidents on this course, and in 1935 the organizing authorities took precautions to keep the spectators away from all dangerous points, erecting palisades and building barricades of straw bales.

During the afternoon one car, while being braked to a stop, slid sideways and struck a tree, bursting into flames; the driver, however, managed to escape from the machine uninjured. Up to that time four new records had been established in various classes, and now a new record for the hill was set up by Robert Benoist who, driving a Bugatti, covered the course in 30·4 secs. In braking he, too, skidded badly, but was able to straighten without leaving the road.

Shortly afterwards a racing driver named Cattaneo came up the hill on another Bugatti, and under the action of the brakes short of the finishing line the car spun completely round, sliding off the road into the crowd. With the driver making desperate efforts to right the machine, the car slid the other way, shooting across the road again into the crowd on the opposite side. Three of the spectators were killed instantaneously, another was

MOTOR RACING AND RECORD BREAKING

so badly injured that he died later, and more than twenty others had to be rushed to hospital. Fortunately such accidents are rare, and in this case it resulted in a full review of the regulations governing hill climbs in France.

Hill climbing, as a phase of motor racing, places a premium upon acceleration, and helps to develop machines which can get away from a standing start very rapidly. At the same time, it sets for designers the problem of keeping the car's wheels on the ground, and ensuring that the tyres grip the surface; failing this, wheel-spin results and the machine is slowed.

In 1932 the Bugatti firm produced a car with four-wheel drive, a model of which was used by Robert Benoist at Chateau-Thierry. The primary purpose of this machine was for competition in hill climbs, and it was hoped that its relatively unorthodox design would result in tremendous acceleration. If all four wheels were driving the car, it was obvious that its performance must be better—theoretically, at any rate—than if only two wheels transmitted the power of the engine.

A car such as this is a relatively rare production, and in the main it is not usual for anyone other than an enthusiast to construct a car specially for hill climbs. It has been found that the very high performance of modern road-racing machines makes them ideal for such events. For this reason hill climbing has become an interesting aspect of motor racing, but not one which now contributes very directly or effectively to the industry as a whole.

CHAPTER VIII

RACING IN AMERICA

ALTHOUGH road races were held in the United States more than a quarter of a century ago, American racing has not developed on the lines taken by the sport in Europe; it is almost entirely confined to 'dirt track' events, and to the annual five hundred miles race over brick-paved Indianapolis.

America is the home of dirt-track racing, and the evolution of this sport can easily be traced. Since no built-up tracks were available—other than at Indianapolis—while road races required considerable organization, early events were arranged in which cars ran in a circle over a stretch of fairly level, open ground. As the grass was worn away, the earth was bared and a 'dirt'-surfaced course was produced. In order to make this more durable, cinders were sometimes strewn on it, thus beginning the form which modern American 'dirt tracks' have taken.

These courses are usually about one mile in circumference, and the events are highly spectacular. The old tracks, many of which are still in use, have no banking, and the drivers often go through the curves in one long skid. The speeds on such tracks cannot normally be very high, owing to the limitations of the circuit, but races can easily be followed by the spectators, who have the whole circuit in view.

About twenty years ago these flat courses began to give place to 'board tracks,' which remained peculiar to America. These were specially constructed, and being surfaced with wooden planks proved very smooth, while steep banking made them remarkably fast in spite of the fact that all were a mile, or one mile and a quarter in circumference.

Board tracks made possible the achievement of really amazing average speeds over long distances, and the fastest course of all was undoubtedly that at Atlantic City, New Jersey. This track was opened in January 1926, and the inaugural race was three hundred miles in length; it was won by Harry Hartz at a speed of 134·1 m.p.h., the feat being performed with a two-litre Miller car. Later on Frank Lockhart set up a lap record on this track with 147 m.p.h.

One of the features of board-track racing is that a number of cars are on the course at the same time, all travelling very rapidly, and when a dozen machines are in action on a course hardly more than a mile in length, it is obvious that the cars must occasionally become bunched. When that happened drivers found themselves moving literally wheel to wheel, and at speeds often much in excess of 120 m.p.h., the life of each man dependent upon the skill and the nerve of his immediate rivals.

This helped to draw very large crowds to the new speedways, because they offered even greater excitement than that obtainable at dirt-track meetings. The result was the rapid appearance of a large number of board tracks, staging events which invariably drew crowds numbering between twenty and thirty thousand people. Four courses appeared in California—at Fresno, Beverley Hills, San Carlos, and Cotati—and two more were opened in that state in 1924; one of these was just south of San Francisco, and the other was at Culver City, where the initial event produced an average speed of 126·9 m.p.h.

79 ALTOONA SPEEDWAY, PENNSYLVANIA, A BOARD TRACK. THIS VIEW SHOWS ONE OF THE VERY SHORT STRAIGHTS, AND THE INFIELD OF SMOOTH EARTH

HALFWAY ROUND THE TRACK IN THE OPENING LAP OF AN AMERICAN DIRT TRACK EVENT

for two hundred and fifty miles. Other tracks came into existence at Kansas City and Altoona, in Pennsylvania, Laurel City and Salem, and at Charlotte, North Carolina. By 1926 hardly a race was being run off at less than two miles a minute.

A difficulty developed with board tracks, however. Oil dropped by the cars affected the plank surfacing, hot sunshine and rain made the woodwork warp and, in addition, the action of tyres created holes. Even in 1922, courses which had first been built began to wear out, and one at Uniontown, Pennsylvania, developed so many holes during a long-distance race that the track was abandoned. A month later the same thing happened to the board track at Tacoma, Washington, and in 1924 the course at Kansas City reached such a state of disintegration half-way through a race that the cars had to be stopped.

As time passed track after track gave out and fell into desuetude until, by 1931, only the course at Altoona was in use. This, after a life of eight years, had begun to splinter and break up, and has not since figured in the chief American events.

The high speeds of the cars on board tracks, and the closeness at which the machines ran, made such work very dangerous, and America lost many of her finest drivers. Roscoe Sarles, Howard Wilcox, Joe Boyer, and Fred Comer were all killed in bad crashes, but the worst smash of all was that at Altoona Speedway in June 1929, when seven cars piled into one another.

The race had been scheduled for two hundred miles, and three-quarters of this distance had been run—with the leading car averaging 119 m.p.h.—when a machine skidded into the guard-rail at the top of the banking, bounced off and spun backwards across the course, traversing the path of following cars.

The driver immediately in rear was Ray Keech, at one time holder of the world's land-speed record. He was riding high on the banking and, in endeavouring to avoid the wreck, he also hit the guard-rail, tearing away a great section of it. This woodwork slid down across the course, while Keech's car skidded wildly and overturned, slithering along the centre of the track and finally coming to rest at the foot of the banking.

One of the cars behind him struck his machine, hurtling into the air in a somersault and crashing beyond. A fourth car—its driver striving to avoid the smashed machines before him—hit the broken guard-rail, skidded for some distance, then charged into the open ground on the inside of the track. A fifth machine hit one of the wrecks, but, although it was badly damaged, the driver remained unhurt. A sixth car, driven by Louis Meyer, hit the rail which had fallen to the track and lost its front axle, while the driver of the seventh machine, in trying to stop, skidded broadside along the track, hit the broken fence and slid to a halt. This series of crashes occurred with calamitous rapidity. Three of the drivers were very seriously injured, and Keech was killed instantaneously, while the race was abandoned.

The history of board-track racing is marked by smashes, and it is possible that the risks which drivers ran actually contributed to the fact that some of the courses eventually found difficulty in attracting spectators, and this phase of American racing began to fade. This came about in spite of the fact that some organizers offered large sums in prize-money, often as much as four thousand pounds, for a race of two hundred miles. As the tracks began to wear, and the crowds dwindled, it was impossible to provide money for the upkeep of the courses; repairs became more and more necessary as time passed until, finally, the board speedways were abandoned and a revival of dirt-track racing followed.

The revival was assisted by the fact that a new type of dirt course was constructed, built with banked curves which could be taken without need for skidding, while a hard-packed surface was provided instead of a loose one. This resulted in far higher speeds than had been achieved on the old tracks, and such circuits have now risen to a level of popularity which matches that of the board tracks at their best.

The cars employed in the more important events are usually either Miller or Duesenberg machines, these being the only true racing cars built in America. In recent years they have been rivalled by reconstructed 'stock' cars, but the original source of the majority of machines in an American race is usually hidden under a name selected by a firm manufacturing accessories or components, and sponsoring the car. Machines run under such names as 'Bowes Seal Special,' 'Boyle Valve Special,' 'Gilmore Special,' 'Simplex Special,' while the car itself might be a Miller or a Duesenberg or a 'stock' machine prepared for racing.

All racing is strictly governed by the American Automobile Association, which issues sanctions for the various tracks, and organizes a National Championship. Drivers score points for the championship in the various events in which they take part, and their efforts to secure the national title result in very keen duels, on courses which may be wide apart.

The A.A.A. control is very necessary, because America has a large number of 'outlaw' dirt tracks. These are not under the jurisdiction of the Association, and are usually small and of indifferent design. On these courses, however, new drivers endeavour to gain sufficient experience to qualify for a competition permit from the A.A.A., and enter big events. Such a driver is usually asked to prove his ability over the track on which he wishes to make his debut; he is watched by experienced men, and is further required to cover the circuit within a definite margin of the lap record. Even though he may do well in this test, he does not actually receive his permit unless his performance in the race itself is satisfactory. These precautions are very necessary, because dirt-track work calls for skill, and big events are fought out at such speed that the lives of other drivers would be endangered by a man who lacked real ability in handling his car.

There are now indications that road racing will revive in America. Minor events were held during 1934, and December of that year saw an altogether more important race over a road-type course at Mines Field Aerodrome, near Los Angeles. The circuit is shaped very much like a letter 'B,' the upright stroke forming the grandstand straightaway, but the length of the course is only about one and a half miles.

The December event was a two hundred miles race for 'stock' cars, and fog during the morning left the circuit so damp that the wheels of the machines kicked mud behind, and this, lodging in the radiators of following cars, was responsible for overheating, causing delay and some retirements amongst the twenty machines which started.

The race was won by Kelly Petillo, who had already gained a reputation for daring. Some fifty thousand spectators were present, and Petillo secured £700 in

81 PASSING THE GRANDSTAND DURING A 100-MILES RACE ON THE LANGHORNE DIRT TRACK, PENNSYLVANIA

82 IN ACTION FOR THE MIDGET CAR CHAMPIONSHIP RACE, CALIFORNIA. THE LEADING MACHINE WON THE 75-MILES EVENT AT AN AVERAGE OF 36·2 M.P.H.

83 MIDGET CARS IMMEDIATELY AFTER THE START IN AN OUTDOOR RACE, LOS ANGELES

prize-money, after winning at an average speed of 77·9 m.p.h. His car was known as a 'Gilmore Special,' and the nature of the short road circuit—more arduous, in some respects, than any Continental course—makes his speed the more surprising.

It is likely that the success of racing at Mines Field will see a development of this type of event, but, in the meantime, America is responsible for a new and altogether different style of motor racing. Events have been organized for what are known as 'midget' cars; these are quite small, often running over indoor tracks, and the machines are anything but midgets in speed and power. Their engines are usually about 1,500 c.c., and most of the machines are capable of at least 75 m.p.h., while over 100 m.p.h. has actually been achieved.

These speeds are not possible in actual racing, because the cars compete on unbanked, oval, dirt-surfaced courses with a lap length of under 400 yards. According to design, the cars weigh between five and seven hundredweight, and take part in events which last for twenty or thirty laps.

'Midget' racing began in 1933, and American interest in it is rapidly increasing. Five new tracks were opened early in 1935 at New York and Chicago, and meetings usually draw some ten thousand spectators. Competing drivers come from some of the dirt tracks, but the new sport does not attract men who participate in important events with true racing machines, and it is unlikely that competition with midget cars will prove more than a passing phase.

American racing has produced a car quite different from that used in Europe, and one which is not seriously employed as a stage in the betterment of motor-cars generally. The spectacular qualities of racing are stressed, the prize-money is very high and everything is sacrificed to speed.

Although cars specially constructed for Indianapolis, and for events which comprise the national championship, are very highly developed vehicles, beautifully built and exceedingly fast, at the same time there is little indication that racing practice, as revealed by these machines, is turned to quick account by the manufacturers of normal cars—as constantly occurs in Europe.

American race drivers themselves must rank amongst the finest in the world. The form that their sport has taken necessitates extreme skill and courage, and that they could hold their own with European drivers is suggested by the fact that, in 1921, Jimmy Murphy brought over a Duesenberg and won the French Grand Prix. As a corollary to this, Peugeot cars—made in France—have three times won the Indianapolis race, the last time being in 1919, while a German-built Mercédès also won there in 1915.

The chief reason why Americans rarely compete in Europe is because the necessary journey is so long, and the expense so great, that even outright victory in an important road race would hardly be sufficient to meet the cost involved. Whether a specially built American racing machine could hold its own against the modern Alfa-Romeo, Auto-Union, and Mercédès cars is a matter which could be settled only by actual trial. But if America did produce such a machine, it is certain that she could also produce men capable of handling it.

CHAPTER IX
ENDURANCE RACING

In 1923 a French automobile club decided to organize a road race which was to last for twenty-four hours; they planned a start at four o'clock on Saturday afternoon, the cars running all through the night until the same hour on Sunday. The object of the event was to prove the road-worthiness of the competing machines, the race being open to sports cars in touring trim, as distinct from stripped Grand Prix racing machines.

The organizers were doubtful concerning the popularity of such a long event and, for the amusement of spectators who might temporarily lose interest in the cars, various sideshows were arranged, including a fireworks display, a dance-hall and a cocktail bar, while special arrangements were made to relay wireless concerts from Paris.

The event was run off over the Sarthe circuit, just outside Le Mans, and ended in victory for a Chenard-Walcker, which averaged 57·1 m.p.h. for the twenty-four hours. The only English machine in the race was a Bentley, entered by Captain J. F. Duff, which tied with a Bignan for fourth place. The race started in a hailstorm, followed by heavy rain which lasted for the first four hours, so that the cars were travelling in showers of fine mud; overnight, the weather cleared, and the race ended in sunshine. It was the first really big event of its type that the world had ever seen, and it created so much attention that it was decided to run the race again the following year.

MOTOR RACING AND RECORD BREAKING

Over forty cars started in what proved to be a most arduous and gruelling event, and only fourteen machines were running at the end. In this year—1924—Captain Duff's Bentley won at an average speed of 53·7 m.p.h. With each successive race, interest increased and the importance of the Grand Prix d'Endurance grew greater, while speeds became higher until, in 1933, the winning car averaged 81·5 m.p.h. for the twenty-four hours.

The race was introduced at a time when manufacturers were finding it hard to support the expense of building special cars for true Grands Prix; they turned their attention to Le Mans, with the result that events held there were soon being run off under conditions of great rivalry. This drew very large crowds, who found it thrilling to watch the fastest of all Continental sports cars travelling at anything up to 120 m.p.h., their headlamps blazing as they roared through the dead of night. The illuminated replenishment pits and lighted grandstand, the camp-fires of spectators beside the course, the many booths and sideshows, helped to make a scene without parallel anywhere in the world.

For four years in succession a British Bentley car won the race against the most intense opposition, and each event was marked by incidents which demonstrated the grim way the race was fought. In 1927 there was an extraordinary succession of crashes during the night, at what is known as White House bend, at a time when a drizzle of rain was falling. A car skidded and hit a wall, sliding outwards again and stopping almost in the centre of the road. One of the Bentley team, following at 90 m.p.h., endeavoured to avoid the wrecked machine and went into the ditch, then a French car, travelling immediately behind, skidded wildly and stopped just beyond the halted machines, but facing in

84 THE START OF THE GRAND PRIX D'ENDURANCE, LE MANS

85 THE LAGONDA WHICH WON THE TWENTY-FOUR HOURS ENDURANCE RACE FOR SPORTS MACHINES AT LE MANS IN 1935

86 DRIVEN BY PHILIPPE ETANCELIN AND LOUIS CHINETTI, THIS ALFA-ROMEO WON THE GRAND PRIX D'ENDURANCE, 1934

the wrong direction. Before the driver could recover, a second Bentley thundered into the turn, missed the first wreck and hit the ditched Bentley with such force that it was hurled back on to the road, the second Bentley taking its place. Two other cars charged into the scattered machines, then the third member of the Bentley team arrived. Its driver, warned by debris on the road, managed to slow sufficiently to avoid charging headlong into the damaged machines. He could not, however, prevent contact with the car which had first skidded and the impact smashed one wheel, a mudguard and one headlamp; the driver carried on, effected repairs at his pit, and eventually won the race.

In such an event it cannot be expected that one driver could handle a car for the entire twenty-four hours, although this has been done. Two drivers are allowed for each car, and the usual procedure is for them to change over each time the machine comes in for replenishment. The Grand Prix d'Endurance is governed by a series of very stringent regulations, all parts of the car being under lead seals during the race, the whole object of which is thoroughly to test the reliability of the machines. The nature of the circuit itself ensures this.

From the starting-point at the grandstand, the road curves into a series of S-bends, beyond which it turns abruptly on to a long straight which is so wide that it has the appearance almost of being a section from some racing track. This ends in a deceptive dip before Mulsanne corner, around which the course continues by a narrow road running between thick pine woods. A second set of sharp S-bends at the end of this brings the course to another corner, the road continuing narrow and winding as far as White House bend, with the grandstand a little distance beyond.

In recent years this bend has been eased off, largely as a result of crashes which have occurred here, but more particularly because of a series of ugly smashes during the race of 1933. On the first lap a car which was endeavouring to hold the pace of the leaders skidded, rammed the bank and turned completely upside down. Its wreckage was left in the ditch, and two hours later another car—entering the White House bend too fast, skidded and wrecked itself, while a machine which was following also went off the road in trying to avoid the sliding car in front. Men were clearing away the debris when the wreckage of the car which had been first to crash was struck by still another machine, so that four cars lay wrecked within a distance of fifty yards, although in no case was anyone seriously hurt.

The great keenness of competing drivers was very largely the cause of these accidents, and the Grand Prix d'Endurance is always very closely fought out. An instance of this is offered by the 1933 event. Tazio Nuvolari, driving an Alfa-Romeo, held the lead on the last lap, when his brakes had lost their power; ten yards behind him was Chinetti on a similar car. He followed Nuvolari down the road into the S-bends, then snatched the lead on the turn into the straight. He lost it during the fast run towards Mulsanne corner but, by virtue of his superior brakes, regained it immediately before the turn.

If Nuvolari was to win he had to pass again before they entered the next set of S-bends at Arnage. He opened flat out through the pine woods, travelling with his wheel-hubs all but brushing the wattle fencing which, at this point, holds back the spectators. He managed to pass, and held the lead through the bends, remained in front through the corner beyond and held Chinetti off during the dash to White House and the finish. Nuvolari won by only ten seconds, after an event which had lasted for twenty-four hours, and was the fastest ever run at Le Mans.

The success of the Grand Prix d'Endurance naturally brought about the organization of similar races, one of the most notable being the Belgian Grand Prix de Vingt-Quatre Heures. This event is run off over a road circuit near Spa, the course being 9·3 miles in length and set in a valley. The race is for sports machines, and the circuit is not so fast as at Le Mans. Louis Chiron, partnered by Chinetti, won there in 1933 at an average speed of 72·6 m.p.h., this being the highest pace ever recorded for the twenty-four hours. In 1934 the race was changed to a ten-hours' event, when a Bugatti averaged 72·8 m.p.h. for that time.

A similar endurance race was organized at Brooklands, and became known as the 'Double-Twelve.' Since it is not permissible to run cars for the full twenty-four hours at the track, the machines travelled for twelve hours on one day, then were removed from the course and placed under an official guard, the drivers taking the cars over again and bringing them to the line for a re-start the following morning. No attention could be given to the machines overnight and the event was—but for the break in the race—run under much the same regulations as at Le Mans.

It was held for three years in succession, and in 1930 was won by a Bentley at a speed of 86·6 m.p.h. The next race was won by an M.G. Midget, with four other cars of the same *marque* following this machine home. The Double-Twelve then gave place to a Thousand Miles endurance event, in which cars ran for five hundred miles each day, but the race was not altogether successful and was held only once. It was, in any case, completely overshadowed by another thousand miles event: the Mille Miglia. This is held in Italy and is a successor to the old-style town-to-town races.

The Mille Miglia was first projected in 1926, and the opening race was held in 1927. A course was selected which began at Brescia, not far from Milan, then ran down through the centre of Italy to Bologna and Florence, reaching as far southward as Rome. Here, the circuit turned out to the coast of the Adriatic sea, running up to the Venetian Alps before heading back to Brescia again. The course is sometimes changed in detail from year to year, but its main outlines remain the same, while the distance is always a little in excess of one thousand miles, usually about twenty miles more.

When entries for the event were first invited there were many prognostications of disaster. The old Paris-Madrid was the last such race which had been held, and, obviously, it would not be possible to guard so long a course, or to stop normal traffic making use of it. No less than eighty machines came to the starting line, while excited spectators gathered everywhere along the great circuit.

At Le Mans, cars run over a prepared road course; at Brooklands, in the Double-Twelve, they used an enclosed track, but in Italy they were faced with all the difficulties, the hazards and dangers of quite ordinary roads. At one point, machines had to use a pontoon bridge to cross a river, while everywhere drivers had to

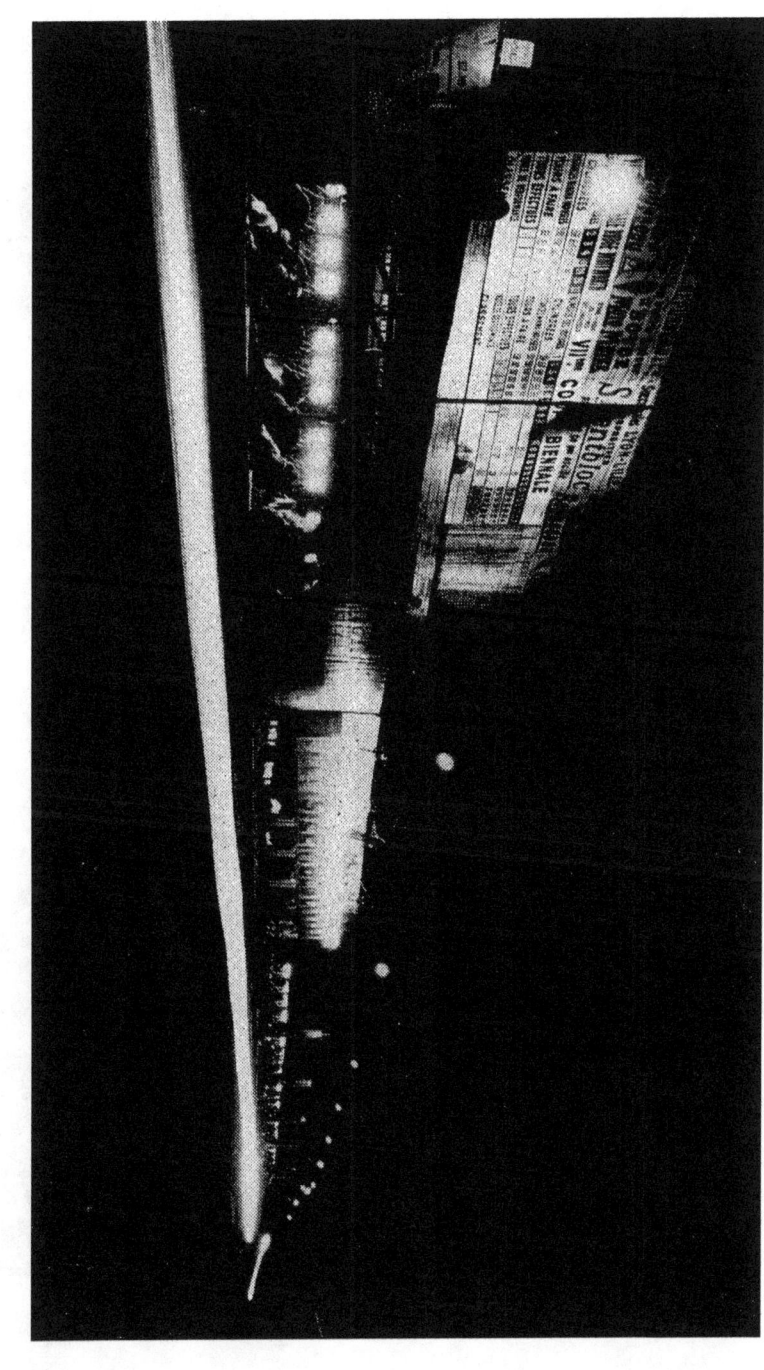

87 DURING THE NIGHT AT LE MANS. THE WHITE STREAK IN THE FOREGROUND WAS MADE BY THE HEADLIGHTS OF CARS AS THEY RACED PAST

88 DRIVERS AND MECHANICS RUNNING TO THEIR MACHINES AT THE OPENING OF A BROOKLANDS 'DOUBLE-TWELVE' RACE

rely upon signs and indicators in order to keep on the right course. Difficulties of illuminating these during the night hours were overcome by spectators, who lit bonfires on the corners, or employed the headlamps of their cars to show the route.

From start to finish, the race lasted more than twenty-one hours, and the winning machine averaged 48·6 m.p.h. over dangerous mountain roads and dusty plains, through towns and remote villages. The Mille Miglia was a complete success, and preparations for the next year's race roused the whole of Italy to an enthusiasm which reached its climax on the day of the event. The distance was covered in nearly two hours less time, and the average speed rose to 53·2 m.p.h. By 1932 the speed had gone up to 68 m.p.h. and in 1934 the winners—Achille Varzi and Bignami—averaged over 70 m.p.h. and finished the course in 14 hours 8 minutes 5 seconds.

Consideration of these speeds is sufficient to demonstrate the value of this type of event. In the course of eight races the pace had lifted from 48 to 71 m.p.h., while the time for the distance had been shortened by one-third. The 1934 race began at four o'clock in the morning in pouring rain, the machines starting with their headlamps blazing. It was still raining when they reached the point where the course ran through the Raticosa pass, limiting visibility badly and persisting until the machines in the lead had crossed the Futa pass farther on. Persistent mist made matters yet more difficult; not far from Florence, Lord Howe, who was driving an M.G. Magnette, skidded into a wall, then struck a telegraph pole, which split and broke at the impact.

The rain stopped as the leaders reached Rome and

turned north-east, only for the weather conditions to become bad again when they reached Bologna. Rain fell during all the remaining two hundred and thirty-five miles to the finishing point and, in view of these conditions, the speeds set up by the leading machines form a great tribute to the skill of their drivers.

That cars could average far more than a mile a minute over unprepared roads, through rain and mist, travelling by mountain highways and through towns is full proof of their stability and road-worthiness.

Such endurance racing is as great a test of men as of machines. In the Le Mans event one driver remains at the pit, while his partner handles the car; in the Mille Miglia, however, both drivers travel on the machine, one exchanging seats with the other at predetermined points.

On so long a course it is difficult for any man to memorize the whole of the road, and the usual practice is for a driver to make himself familiar with certain sections, and take the car over these, his companion having done his best to become acquainted with other portions of the course. In the event of a breakdown, repairs must be effected with whatever spare parts and tools there may be on the car, unless the machine can reach one of the replenishment depots which are generally set up at the main controls.

These depots are placed at strategic points, and usually depend upon the petrol consumption of the car concerned. A machine with a petrol consumption of one gallon to every fifteen miles, and a petrol tank holding twenty gallons, would establish a depot at about two hundred and fifty miles from the starting-point; this would bring the car in with a balance of three gallons

89 DURING THE TARGA ABRUZZO, AN ENDURANCE RACE AT PESCARA, ITALY. LORD HOWE IS CORNERING WITH AN ALFA-ROMEO

90 IN WINNING THE 'DOUBLE-TWELVE' RACE AT BROOKLANDS IN 1930, THIS BENTLEY AVERAGED 86·6 M.P.H. AND COVERED 2,080 MILES IN THE TWENTY-FOUR HOURS

91 CARS LEAVING AT THE START OF THE BOL D'OR, A TWENTY-FOUR HOURS ROAD RACE RUN OFF NEAR PARIS

ENDURANCE RACING

of fuel, when the tank would be replenished and the machine would run on to its next depot. The regulations permit a replenishment pit to be placed at almost any point of the course, so that the Mille Miglia sees hastily formed depots at the roadside in nearly every town after the mountains have been crossed on the way to Rome.

In effect, the machines have to run almost entirely without outside assistance, drivers making repairs or changing deflated wheels wherever they happen to be brought to a stop. Such a race is a very great strain, since there cannot be any respite. Because of this, the Mille Miglia finds a parallel almost only in what was once a very famous race—the Targa Florio. This event has now lost much of its prestige, but the race remains in history as a very great test of endurance, and may yet be restored to its old popularity.

The Targa Florio is run over the Madonie circuit in Sicily, the course consisting almost entirely of mountain roads. At times it has been necessary to alter the planned circuit as a result of land-slides. The race was originated in 1906, when a circuit over ninety miles in length was employed, but after the war this was shortened to one of just under seventy miles. It has been calculated that, on each lap, over fifteen hundred corners have to be taken, which accounts for the fact that the race has never been won at more than 48·7 m.p.h.

It is impossible to employ a massed start over such a course, and cars leave the line at intervals, at once starting a climb from sea-level to the village of Cerda. After this the road becomes still more steep, travelling by endless corners and turns to Caltavuturo, in the heights beyond which bandits hid in the days when the initial Targa Florio races were run.

MOTOR RACING AND RECORD BREAKING

From this point the circuit climbs yet higher, becoming at times only a ledge on the side of a mountain. In some of the villages the road is only wide enough to accommodate a single machine, having been built for pack-mules rather than for automobiles, and not until the cars regain sea-level—at Campofelice—is a straight stretch reached. This lasts for five miles, and brings the course back to its starting-point. The potential speed of the cars and the dangerous nature of the course, coupled with the intense rivalry of drivers, makes the Targo Florio a very severe race, and a definite test of endurance.

The only other really important endurance race is the Giro d'Italia which, although as yet held but once—in 1934—is the world's longest event, since it involves a circuit covering the whole of Italy, with a length of some 3,530 miles.

The race was organized for unsupercharged sports cars, and was split into three stages. The first stage began at the Littorio track, outside Rome, from which the cars ran down through Naples, crossed the Messina Straits and raced around Sicily back to Messina, a distance of 1,080 miles. After one day's rest, the machines travelled up to Milan, covering 1,235 miles, and the third stage involved a circuitous route back to Rome completing the total distance with another 1,217 miles.

The event was most arduous, and nearly forty of the two hundred starters fell out during the first stage, the race ending in a victory for a Lancia car, which averaged 51·7 m.p.h. over the distance. In some measure the race was successful; but possibly because the event is somewhat unwieldy and difficult to organize, the Giro d'Italia has not been held since.

92 AN M.G. MAGNETTE, WITH COUNT LURANI AT THE WHEEL, RACING IN THE MILLE MIGLIA, A THOUSAND-MILES EVENT OVER ITALIAN ROADS

93 THE WINNERS OF THE MILLE MIGLIA RACE IN 1935, PINTACUDA AND DELLA STUFA

94 THIS ALFA-ROMEO SKIDDED AND CRASHED DURING THE GRAND PRIX D'ENDURANCE AT LE MANS. THE DRIVER WAS THROWN CLEAR WHEN THE CAR HIT THE BROKEN TREE IN THE FOREGROUND

ENDURANCE RACING

Endurance races of this type may be regarded as a final test of adaptations and improvements suggested by true Grands Prix and similar events. It is at Le Mans and over the Mille Miglia circuit that opportunity is offered for practical work, under conditions far more exacting than any which the machine is likely to endure in the hands of an ordinary owner.

For this reason endurance events have a definite place in the calendar of motor racing and one which, in all probability, they will hold for a long time to come.

CHAPTER X

RACING RISKS

It is an axiom of motor racing that a driver's first duty is to keep his car on the road. The reason is very easy to appreciate when it is realized that the moment a car leaves the course it is out of its element, a danger to its driver and to anyone in the vicinity.

The risks of racing exist in three forms only. There is the chance of some mechanical failure bringing about an accident, the possibility of intervention by some agency outside the car itself, and there is the chance of misjudgment upon the part of the driver. It is safe to assert that every crash, whether with serious results or not, may be attributed to one of these three causes.

One of the most remarkable instances of mechanical failure in motor-racing history occurred during the French Grand Prix of 1922. This was a race over a distance of 499 miles for cars of 1,500 c.c., and was held on a triangular road circuit at Strasbourg, with a lap distance of 8·3 miles. Eighteen cars lined up, after weeks of excitement and preparation, and amongst these machines was a team of three Italian cars.

These were beautifully built, red-painted machines specially prepared for the race. They dominated the event from the start, and it was not very long before they were lapping at 80 m.p.h., leading the race. A driver named Felice Nazarro was in front; it was nearly sixteen years since he had actively competed in road racing, and he had come from his retirement to lead

RACING RISKS

the team. Behind him was Pietro Bordino and Biagio Nazarro, nephew of Felice.

With only four laps to go, and when the three Italian cars were nearly an hour ahead of their nearest rivals, Biagio Nazarro was travelling flat out along a straight stretch when he lost his near-side rear wheel. The car swung completely round and struck a tree; it leaped from this to the centre of the road, turning upside down, bouncing twice more before it came to a stop by a ditch. The driver was flung to the far side of the highway, while the mechanic fell close to the car; he was not badly hurt, but Biagio Nazarro died shortly after he was picked up.

Pietro Bordino—the second member of the team—twice passed the smoking wreck then, when he was about to enter his last lap, the near-side rear wheel also flew from his machine. Fortunately, however, the car did not capsize, but came safely to rest without injury to driver or mechanic, although it slid wildly and rammed a bank.

The cause of the two crashes was the same. In each case the rear axle casing fractured close against the hub. The second accident occurred just about the time that Felice Nazarro was taking the remaining car across the finishing line, to win the race at an average speed of 79·2 m.p.h., precisely ten miles an hour faster than the next car home. It was said that a crack was visible in the axle casing of his machine when the car was examined after the race. Had there been two or three more laps to cover, it is possible that this car might also have fallen out.

The mishaps were clear instances of mechanical failure, and could not possibly have been foreseen. The weak part was, of course, immediately strengthened in future cars and they afterwards enjoyed a long period of outstanding successes. They were, in design and construction, a long way ahead of their rivals, as following events proved, while the crashes were typical of those quite unavoidable risks which must always be associated with racing.

Motor racing can produce many similar instances, and it is always a vital necessity to guard against what is known as 'fatigue' in metal. After prolonged strain, metal has a tendency to develop flaws, and this is the reason why the front axles and steering mechanism on racing cars are kept bright and free from paint. Any crack can then instantly be detected.

Nowadays it is very rarely that the transmission fails in such a way as to put the car out of control, because metals have so greatly improved. The kind of thing that used sometimes to happen is illustrated by a tragic occurrence on Pendine Sands, when J. G. Parry Thomas was killed in attempting to set up a new world's record with his great car, 'Babs.'

This machine had an aero-engine with a cubic capacity of over 27,000 c.c., giving off about 400 h.p., and the car had originally belonged to Count Louis Zborowski. Thomas had rebuilt the machine, fitting it with a streamlined body, and had already reached over 170 m.p.h. when he took the car to Carmarthenshire at the end of February 1927 with the object of trying still further to improve his speed. At this particular time Segrave was on his way to Daytona with the 1,000 h.p. Sunbeam, hoping to reach 200 m.p.h., and Thomas wanted to break the existing record before Segrave reached America.

'Babs' was a gigantic car for those days, and driving chains were used; such chains had been employed on the old-time Grand Prix cars and on record-breaking

95 ON LEGION ASCOT SPEEDWAY, A CALIFORNIA DIRT TRACK. THE MACHINES IN THE FOREGROUND ARE SKIDDING AS A RESULT OF EFFORTS BY THEIR DRIVERS TO AVOID THE CRASHING CAR AHEAD

96 ONE OF THE MOST EXTRAORDINARY OF ALL MOTOR-RACING PHOTOGRAPHS. THESE TWO CARS RAN OUT OF CONTROL ON THE WOODBRIDGE DIRT TRACK, NEW JERSEY. THE REARMOST MACHINE CRASHED DOWN ON THE OTHER, BUT BOTH DRIVERS ESCAPED SERIOUS INJURY

97 THIS CAR CRASHED IN THE TOURIST TROPHY RACE, 1934

machines, and were, in fact, also being used on the big Sunbeam.

Thomas made four trial runs, and it was during a fifth effort that he approached the measured mile at about 160 m.p.h. The machine was still accelerating when, suddenly, 'Babs' pitched into a tremendous skid, leaped in a wild somersault and landed back on its wheels again, then spun in a great half-circle and finally stopped, bursting into flames. Onlookers rushed to the spot, and the blaze was swiftly extinguished, when it was found that the driver was dead in his cockpit.

One of the driving chains had snapped at a time when the wheel must have been turning at the rate of something very close to two thousand revolutions per minute. The broken end of the chain, tearing through the thin aluminium cover which shrouded it, had whirled upwards, catching Thomas on the head and killing him instantaneously, robbing the motor-racing world of a courageous man who was, at the same time, a very clever engineer.

The smash was almost certainly caused by some failure of the chain itself, and news of the accident reached Segrave by wireless. When he arrived at Daytona, the driving chains on his Sunbeam were carefully scrutinized, but they appeared sound and, eventually, the car achieved the distinction of being the first machine to travel at above 200 m.p.h.

The wreckage of 'Babs' was buried in the sand at Pendine.

No racing car ever diverges from its course without some cause but, occasionally, no amount of investigation will accurately reveal what happened. As a result, crashes do occur in a way which seems mysterious.

MOTOR RACING AND RECORD BREAKING

At the Linas-Montlhéry track during mid-December 1932 an Italian driver named Ruggieri was making an attempt on the world's one-hour record. He was travelling at about 135 m.p.h. when the car ran out of control as it came off the west banking. It swerved, dived to the inside of the track, and flung Ruggeri out. The machine then turned over three times more, finally stopping just in front of the replenishment pits. The car was upside down, and was very badly damaged, and its driver died in hospital a couple of hours later.

At the time of the accident Ruggeri was on his thirteenth lap, but beyond the superstitious possibilities of this circumstance, no cause could be ascribed to the accident. The tyres were intact, and the machine was proved to be mechanically sound. The only possible reason for the smash seems to exist in the fact that some drivers found difficulty in safely bringing a car off the west banking, where the contour of the concrete appeared to give a machine a tendency to swerve. Although this was not experienced by every driver, perhaps Ruggieri became a victim of this particular feature of the track. No one was ever able to tell.

There was a similar unexplained crash at Brooklands in September 1924 when Dario Resta—a world-famous driver who had been extremely successful in American events—was attempting to break records. He had made three laps, and entered the railway straight at 112 m.p.h., with his car travelling steadily and safely. Half-way along this stretch, the machine swerved abruptly to the right, breaking through the corrugated iron fencing which stands between the track and the foot of a railway embankment, coming to a halt in a smother of smoke and flame.

When watchers ran to the spot, the mechanic appeared

98 AFTER CRASHING INTO THE FENCE AT LEGION ASCOT SPEEDWAY, AND OVERTURNING, THIS DRIVER ESCAPED WITH MINOR BRUISES

99 AFTER A SERIES OF SMASHES AT MONZA. NO. 26 BELONGED TO BORZACCHINI, AND THE MACHINE IN THE FOREGROUND WAS DRIVEN BY CASTELBARCO

100 THE WRECKAGE OF GUY MOLL'S MACHINE AFTER LEAVING THE ROAD AT 160 M.P.H. DURING THE COPPA ACERBO

from the smoke, immediately to receive first aid and be rushed to hospital, where it was found that he was not badly hurt. Dario Resta was discovered lying in the long grass beyond the car, and it was evident that he had been killed instantaneously.

No one could tell what caused this smash. One moment the car had been travelling magnificently; two seconds later it was a wreck. The only feasible explanation was that a security bolt on the off-side tyre had punctured the inner tube, but this could be no more than a theory, gained through investigation of the marks left on the track.

Motor racing holds a number of such unexplained accidents. If the mysteries could be solved, however, the causes would be found in one of the three hazards which every driver has to face, but there is no way of proving whether these two accidents were caused by mechanical failure, the fault of the driver, or by some outside agency against which it is difficult to guard. Typical of the latter was the disastrous series of crashes at the Monza track in September 1933.

During the Monza Grand Prix, Count Trossi was driving a red-painted Duesenberg, a very fast car built in America. The race was being run off in heats, and the car took part in the first of these, proving itself so fast that it was soon challenging the leaders. At the end of four laps the Duesenberg slowed and coasted in to the pits; its crankcase had split, and engine oil had been spilled on the south curve.

Following the car, Guy Moll's Alfa-Romeo ran into the oil and skidded badly, spinning round twice before the driver could regain control. The heat ended with Moll in second place, while Count Czaykowski won the event. Moll warned the officials that the oil on the track was dangerous and, before the second heat began, an attempt was made to sweep it from the course. The crowd waited impatiently and, at last, the second heat started.

In this event two of Italy's finest drivers, the Cavaliere Giuseppe Campari and Umberto Borzacchini were expected to make the pace, and Borzacchini took the lead half-way round the course. He was a few yards ahead of Campari when the cars entered the south curve. Just as Moll had done, Borzacchini ran on to the oil, which had not been swept cleanly away. His machine spun round just as Campari also reached the oil. He made a great effort to miss Borzacchini's machine, but got into a bad slide and shot straight up the low banking and off the track, striking a tree. In the same moment Borzacchini's machine overturned.

Both men were killed, while on the next lap another car—driven by Castelbarco—skidded viciously and was wrecked, although its driver escaped serious injury. Shortly afterwards, a fourth machine slid on the oil; this car was being handled by Barbieri, but he remained unhurt.

The heat ended. The debris was cleared away, and the concrete was swept again, after which the third heat was run off without mishap. The south curve was surveyed once more, and it was obvious that the concrete was in a dangerous condition at this point. Drivers who were eligible to run in the final were warned of this, but all agreed to continue and the deciding event began.

For eight laps Count Stanislaus Czaykowski held the lead, then earlier disasters were again repeated, and he skidded at the point where Campari and Borzacchini had

101 THIS CAR WENT OUT OF CONTROL, TURNED OVER AND BURST INTO FLAMES ON THE SECOND LAP OF THE FIVE HUNDRED MILES RACE AT BROOKLANDS IN 1933

102 WHAT CAN HAPPEN WHEN A CAR RUNS OUT OF HAND AT HIGH SPEED. THIS MACHINE SKIDDED AT 110 M.P.H. ON INDIANAPOLIS SPEEDWAY AND SMASHED THROUGH A GUARD FENCE

103 A NECESSARY PRECAUTION. NURSES IN A FIRST-AID STATION ON THE AVUS TRACK

104 ON A BEND AT WOODBRIDGE SPEEDWAY, NEW JERSEY. THE LOSS OF THE OFFSIDE FRONT WHEEL THREW THE MACHINE INTO A SUCCESSION OF CIRCULAR SKIDS

105 AFTER A CRASH IN BARCELONA, WHEN PETER DE PAOLO WRECKED HIS MILLER DURING THE PENYA RHIN GRAND PRIX

106 A COLLISION WHILE SKIDDING A CURVE ON AN AMERICAN DIRT TRACK. THE CAR ON THE LEFT CONTINUED THE RACE

107 ON THE MINES FIELD ROAD COURSE, LOS ANGELES. THIS CAR ENTERED A CORNER TOO FAST AND TURNED A DOUBLE SOMERSAULT

been killed. His car left the course, turning end over end before it stopped; it then burst into flames which were so fierce that it was impossible for anyone to get near the machine and extricate the driver.

Thus, by a fault which existed in neither man nor machines, the racing world lost three of its finest drivers within the space of one hour. Rain was falling while some of the heats were run off, and the wet state of the track undoubtedly contributed to the dangerous condition of the curve. Fortunately such accidents as this are very rare.

Where the driver himself is responsible for a smash, the cause lies invariably in his misjudgment of the risk he has decided to take, and this kind of mishap usually occurs on a corner.

In all road-type races the organizing authorities make every effort to provide what is known as an 'escape road' at each turn. The sole object of this is to assist a driver who finds himself approaching a corner so fast that it is impossible for him to go through it. Such circumstances may arise because his brakes are losing their power—as a result of much use during earlier laps—or because the driver is being forced to very high speed through the pressure of rivals in the heat of the race.

If a man approaches a corner too fast, and makes use of the escape road, no accident occurs. But it sometimes happens that he may enter the corner before he realizes his speed, then the existence of the escape road cannot save him. To some extent this was the cause of a smash which occurred during the Grand Prix of Tripoli in 1934.

Daring young Piero Taruffi, who was driving a 16-cylinder Maserati, took the lead at the start, lapping at over 120 m.p.h., closely pursued by Chiron, Guy Moll, and Achille Varzi, then regarded as the three finest road-racing drivers on the Continent.

By setting up a record lap on the fourth circuit of the course, Chiron challenged for the lead, with Taruffi doing his utmost to retain it, and both trying to stave off the challenge of Varzi and Moll. On the seventh lap, fighting to maintain his position, Taruffi went into the corner at the end of the grandstand straight at altogether too high a speed. His car left the road, smashed through a fence, and Taruffi was flung out at the back of an ambulance which immediately rushed him to hospital. His injuries kept him in bed for some considerable time, but he was able to resume racing again towards the end of the season.

Taruffi's crash was due to his dashing temperament, and the close manner in which the race was being fought. He simply misjudged the pace of his machine, a very easy thing to do at so high a speed. The event was won by Varzi, who averaged 115·6 m.p.h. Guy Moll finished one-fifth of a second behind him, and Chiron was only thirteen seconds farther back. The difference between the machines was very small when it is considered that the race had lasted nearly three hours, and was over a distance of 325 miles.

Such risks as existed were considerably heightened by the pace at which the race for 1935 was run off. The whole of this event was a long-drawn fight between Mercédès, Auto-Union, and specially built twin-engined Alfa-Romeo cars, every one of which had a potential maximum speed of at least 180 m.p.h.

During practice, von Stuck lapped at 137·7 m.p.h. with his Auto-Union, as against the 1934 lap record of 124·5 m.p.h., while Nuvolari took his twin-engined

108 ON THE NORTH CURVE, INDIANAPOLIS. TO THE RIGHT OF THE CRASHING MACHINE IS A HOLE IN THE RETAINING WALL, MADE BY ANOTHER CAR DURING QUALIFYING TRIALS FOR THE RACE

109 A SKID THROUGH THE FENCE DURING THE 500 MILES RACE AT BROOKLANDS, 1934. THE DRIVER WAS SHAKEN, BUT NOT BADLY HURT

110 THE LATE SIR HENRY SEGRAVE

Alfa-Romeo over the road circuit at 133·2 m.p.h. and Caracciola on a Mercédès was only 2 m.p.h. slower.

In the race itself the big Alfa-Romeos wore out their tyres rapidly, while nearly all other cars had to make frequent changes; in spite of this, Caracciola won at over 123 m.p.h., averaging this speed for the distance of 325 miles. The event was marred by an accident to Antonio Brivio; he was struck on the head by a stone flung back from another car, with the result that he lost control of his machine and crashed.

Accidents in motor racing can occur with such overwhelming suddenness that a driver's reactions must be immediate and spontaneous if he is to avert disaster. However, in view of the enormous mileage covered by racing cars during the course of a single season, the proportion of mishaps is very low. In the 1935 Tripoli race, the competing machines must—including practice work—have covered a total of well above 10,000 miles between them, every mile of that distance at an average considerably above 100 m.p.h. Brivio's crash was the only one, and that was caused neither through the car itself nor any fault of its driver.

The failure of some vital part of a machine—resulting in the car going out of control—is now very unusual. An accident caused by the intervention of something outside the car is a chance which has to be faced in any sport. Broadly speaking, this leaves as the only definite hazard the chance of misjudgment on part of the driver himself, but he makes his own risks, and he alone is able to decide whether the risks are too great.

CHAPTER XI

PERSONALITIES

It is very evident that a driver who has the temperament required for success in road racing does not necessarily score in track work, while the man who achieves fame in hill climbs may be a failure at record breaking. This does not always apply, because there are drivers who have gained victories in almost every branch of motor sport, but men do have a tendency to specialize—or, rather, to find that they are more successful in one particular aspect of racing.

The reason is not difficult to understand. In modern road racing a driver has no need to know very much about the technical details of his car; this is not suggesting that some 'crack' drivers have no engineering knowledge, because most of them possess it to a great degree, but it is a fact that such knowledge is secondary in road work.

Nowadays a driver secures a winning position only by gaining fractions of time from his rivals—men as experienced and as skilful as himself. The driver faces risk of disaster if his calculation is wrong by so much as the fifth of a second, and since the men striving against him are equally aware of the need for clipping seconds, the situation presented is one in which skill and judgment count tremendously. There is no room for recklessness, and—all things being equal—success comes to the man who has the greater courage and nerve and dash.

Road racing, then, calls for a particular mentality and temperament and, because of its nature, a driver actually

111 SIR MALCOLM CAMPBELL

112 LOUIS CHIRON

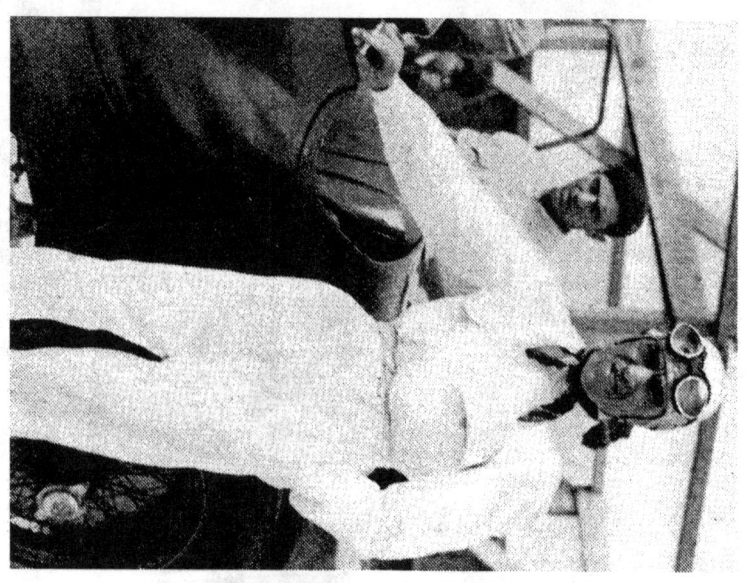

113 TAZIO NUVOLARI

has little time in which to consider his machine. He knows, of course, the limit to which the engine can be pressed, and he knows under what circumstances he will put undue strain on his car, but with him the race, as a race, comes first.

Hill climbing is very different. Here a driver is alone on the road, with nothing to think about except his machine, and the course in front of him. Not being harassed by the presence of other cars, he can make certain that he does not press his engine too hard, while his instruments—as well as his ears—tell him the right moment at which to make the gear changes essential to getting the best out of his mount. Hill climbing can be just as exciting as road racing, but it calls for a different kind of skill and for calculation of a different nature. A man who would be flurried by the close presence of other machines in a race can still gain success on a hill, chiefly because he is at liberty to use all the road and can put his car just where he wishes, without having to watch that he does not balk another driver.

Hill climbing, incidentally, provides excellent training for road racing, and quite a number of drivers have graduated from it. It demands some of the essential judgment of road work, and schools a man in cornering technique.

Track racing definitely calls for engineering knowledge if success is to be gained. On a straightaway course a man can very easily exceed the engine revolutions at which his power unit remains happy, and many a road-racing driver, on running over a track for the first time, has 'burst' his engine. No car can be taken around a track at the limit of its speed all the time; something is certain to fail.

A track driver must watch his instruments incessantly,

and he must know the full meaning of what they record. He must also know how to hold his car on to the banking even though another machine is very close beside him, and that calls for a special quality of nerve.

This may be shown more clearly if one considers two cars travelling round the Byfleet banking at Brooklands, one moving at 130 m.p.h. and the second machine coming up to pass at 132 m.p.h. The leading driver will find the second car coming up relatively slowly and gradually, nosing in beside him, and the machines will travel for almost a mile—moving wheel to wheel—before the slightly faster car has drawn ahead. In other words, for something like half a minute the two cars will be hanging together, neither clear of the other. One driver has to keep his machine high, and the other has to hold his car down, while each man is, of course, anxious not to lose any speed.

This kind of thing is not easy. It demands steadiness and sureness on the part of the drivers, and is entirely a matter of cool calculation. There need be no dash, no daring, no important judgment of distance ahead—simply a special technique and a special quality of skill.

Record breaking is again very different, and here true engineering knowledge is required for all except very short-distance events. In this work a man has to drive in such a way that he is getting from his car the best possible performance and the highest possible speed consistent with the record he is attempting. If it be a five-mile effort, then he must run the machine absolutely flat out. If he is trying for a one-hour record, then he must drive the machine at a pace which will eclipse the existing figures, and yet enable the car to stand up to the work for sixty minutes—which can necessitate quite

PERSONALITIES

delicate handling. Should he be out for long-distance records, then he must gain from his car a speed which stresses neither engine nor transmission, and which may actually be well within the maximum pace of the machine; he is thus asked to exercise considerable restraint.

In record work, success is assisted if a driver knows all about his car, particularly in a long-drawn effort when the flicker of a needle against a dial, or an untoward sound, calls for immediate diagnosis of a developing fault which, swiftly remedied, will enable the attempt to continue.

Drivers are further differentiated by something other than individual temperament, and this is the question of finance. There are very many men who have never had the opportunity of revealing their true qualities simply because they have been unable to obtain the right cars. A man who puts an old-type Grand Prix machine into a race against modern cars can become successful only through the most unusual racing luck; his one hope is that experienced eyes will note his skill and someone will lend him a car with which, later, he may win recognition.

Typical of this situation is the case of the late Sir Henry Segrave. Very eager to race seriously, he bought an old Opel which had been built in 1914, and he raced this at Brooklands during 1920. He won several events there, and also proved successful in hill climbs. He had relatively small private resources, and his ambition was to secure recognition by Louis Coatalen, who was responsible for the Sunbeam and the Darracq cars which raced in those days.

Segrave's efforts with the out-of-date Opel gained him a probationary place in the Sunbeam team for 1921. He did very well, and from that he went on to win the

French Grand Prix for England in 1923, then achieved real fame by being the first man to lift the world's land-speed record to above 200 m.p.h.

Segrave was, undoubtedly, unusually gifted as a road-racing driver, but he secured his opportunity to achieve success without the slightest influential support. Entirely unknown, and without adequate finance, he still gained world-wide recognition and, because of this, his career is an encouragement to those drivers who, perhaps, feel themselves overlooked.

It is impossible to deal with the achievements of the long list of famous race drivers, past and present, but the modern counterpart of Segrave is Louis Chiron, and the Continent has no man to compare with him. He served during the war, driving a car for Maréchal Pétain and, afterwards, for Maréchal Foch. He was about eighteen years old when the war ended, and had only the fact that he had been chauffeur to distinguished generals to aid him in search for a career.

Like Segrave, he wanted to become a racing driver, and his career opened in 1923, when he drove in the La Turbie hill climb. He was then twenty-three years of age, and for four years he took part in every event that he found himself able to enter. Then he joined the official Bugatti team and, within another year, was the world's road-racing champion.

Chiron is tall and handsome, and is particularly popular with the French crowds; he was born at Monaco. He drives with finesse and, although he is very cool, he can produce the necessary dash when it is required. He has to his credit a remarkably long list of victories, having secured first place in nearly every important European race. In twelve years of driving Chiron's skill has helped

114 RUDOLF CARACCIOLA

115 ACHILLE VARZI

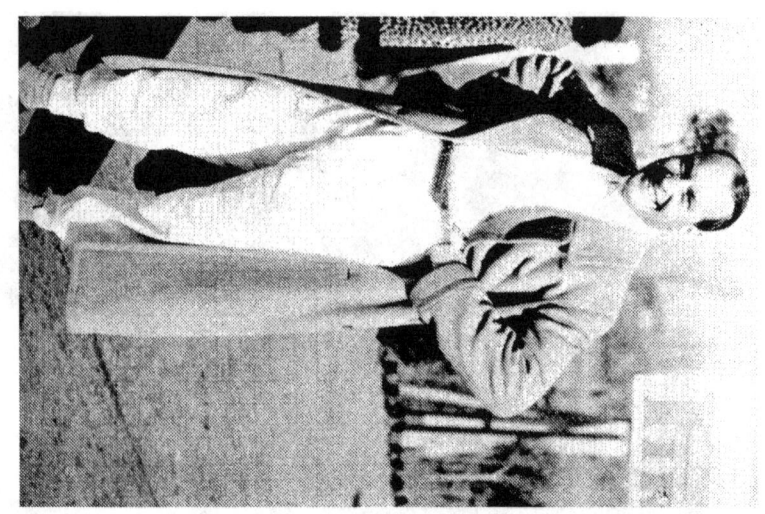

116 HANS VILLIEZ VON STUCK

117 GUY MOLL

PERSONALITIES

him to avoid serious accident, and minor crashes on the Monaco circuit and at Spa are his only mishaps.

Chiron is a typical road-racing driver, and it is now very rarely that he enters for hill climbs. In this respect he is like Segrave, yet both gained much useful early experience in hill climb work.

The careers of Segrave and Chiron find some counterpart in Italy, which has a greater proportion of splendid drivers than any other country in Europe, and where Tazio Nuvolari is regarded as the greatest, with Achille Varzi as almost his match. Both these men began as racing motor-cyclists, and each met with difficulties in finding someone to recognize his ability when he turned to cars.

Nuvolari rode motor-cycles for seven years before he entered his first car race. He is very lightly built—a little man, with small hands and a lean, long chin, who would seem to lack the physique necessary to withstand a long-distance race and to hold a very fast car. Yet he was Italian champion in 1932, and all but secured the title again in 1933. He has won nearly every big Grand Prix at least once, and won the Tourist Trophy in 1930 with an Alfa-Romeo; he was again successful in 1933, with an M.G. Magnette.

He handles a car with the verve usually regarded as fitting to the Italian temperament, and only once has this involved him in difficulties; this was when he crashed badly on the Alessandria circuit, in 1934, but he recovered rapidly from his injuries and was soon racing again.

Achille Varzi's training as a racing motor-cyclist has given him such skill that—in spite of a career which matches Nuvolari's in length—he has never crashed a car. He is altogether bigger, and his temperament is different; outwardly calm, he drives with as much dash as Nuvolari, yet always with a certain caution. His handling of a machine is splendidly controlled and, no matter how fast his approach to a corner, he appears confident and safe and sure.

He won the Italian championship in 1930, and for three years after that he drove Bugattis, then he changed to Alfa-Romeo cars, joining the Ferrari stable, abandoning them for the 1935 season in order to drive the German Auto-Union machines.

None of these men—Chiron, Nuvolari, and Varzi—engages actively in anything except road racing, and in this they are matched by Rudolf Caracciola, a German driver who has raced Mercédès cars almost exclusively since 1923. He is a big, broad-shouldered man with a physique fitting to these great German machines. He has five times won the German Grand Prix, and in 1930 he staggered the Italians by winning the Mille Miglia. In that same year he won the Irish Grand Prix and set up a new record at Shelsley Walsh, and he won the Tourist Trophy in 1929.

His brilliant career received a check through an accident during practice for the Monaco Grand Prix in 1933. He crashed on the Quai de Plaisance, his car striking a wall with such force that, although he was not thrown from the cockpit, he received a compound fracture of the right thigh. He was twelve months in recovering from the injury.

Barely had he regained his health when he was involved in an avalanche at Arosa. He was ski-ing on the slopes of Urdenfurkel, and although he was not greatly hurt he lost his wife, who was with him, and who always took charge of his replenishment depot during a race. Before the 1934 season was ended, however, Caracciola was

118 LUIGI FAGIOLI

119 WHITNEY STRAIGHT

120 BARNEY OLDFIELD

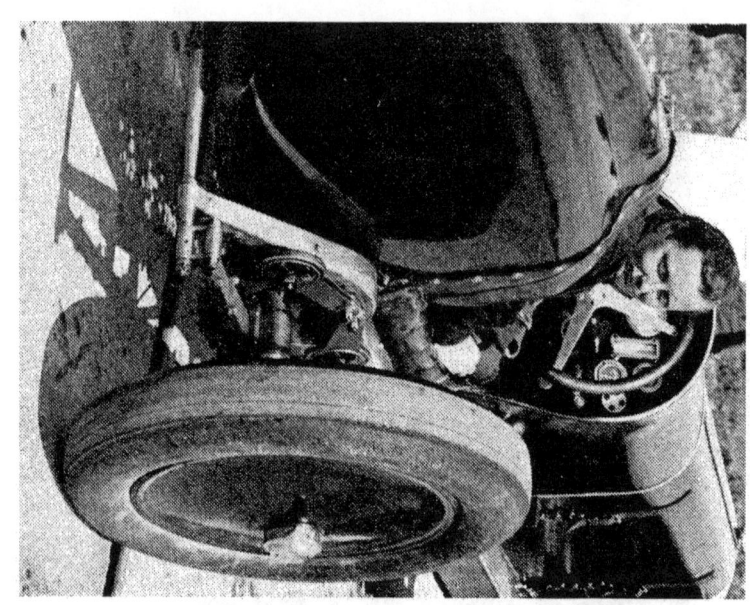

121 MRS. GWENDA STEWART

122 J. G. PARRY THOMAS

123 TOMMY MILTON

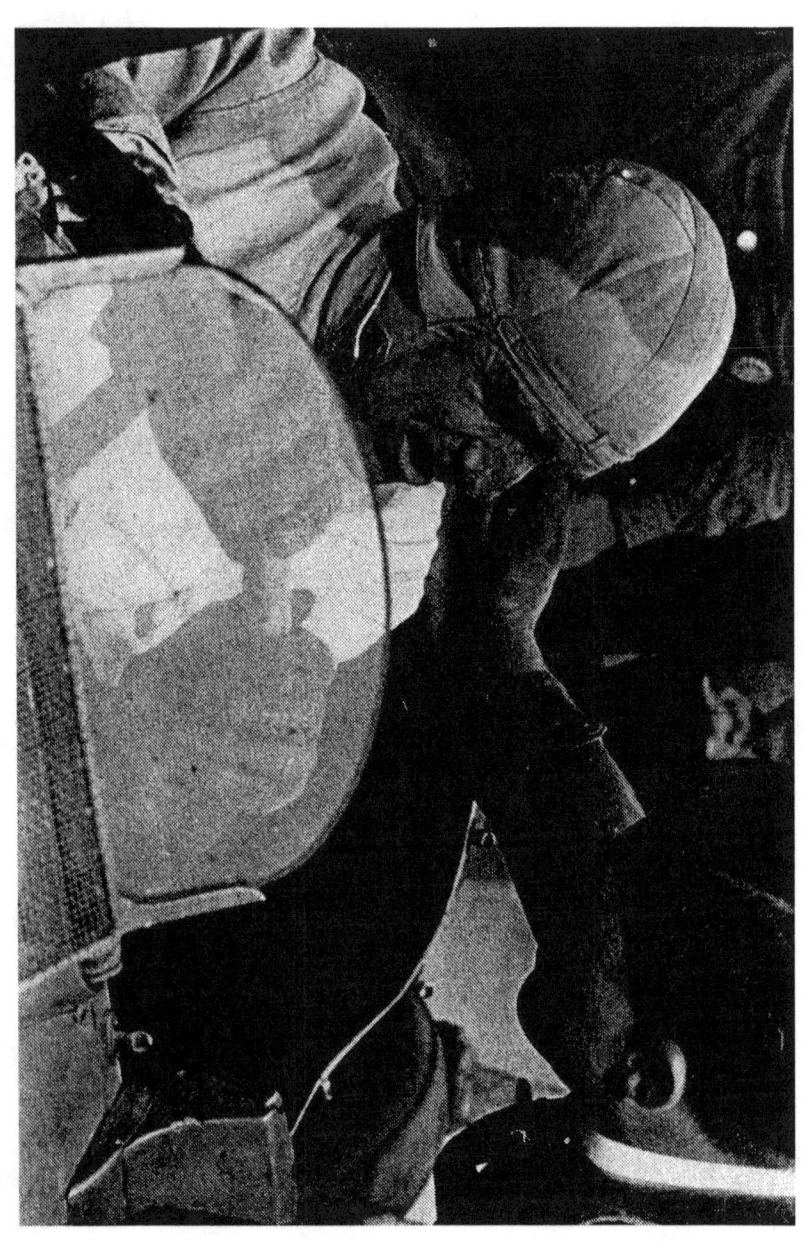

PERSONALITIES

racing again, and in October he turned to record work —but only over very short distances. He created a new class record for the mile by achieving a speed of above 198 m.p.h., using a road-racing Mercédès fitted with a five-litre engine.

Caracciola's great rival during the 1934 and 1935 seasons was an Austrian driver named Hans Villiez von Stuck, driving Auto-Union cars, and von Stuck is an exceptional man. For years he remained as undisputed hill-climb champion of England, having entered this branch of the sport in 1926, when he was thirty-seven years of age. He did not engage in Grand Prix racing until 1934, when he won the German Grand Prix with an Auto-Union at an average speed of 74·1 m.p.h.; this was a record for the race, which was run off over the Nurburg Ring. In this season he also won the Swiss Grand Prix and the Masaryk Grand Prix of Czechoslovakia.

Von Stuck's success both in hill climbing and in road racing is unusual, and he has still further shown his merit by breaking Caracciola's record, and achieving over 199 m.p.h. through the measured mile with an Auto-Union. In the case of both these drivers, however, it should be noted that the very brief dash through the mile is hardly sufficient to establish either as what the French call a *recordman*.

Drivers like von Stuck are exclusively a product of European racing. Attacks on world's and international class records are a rarity in the United States, with the result that America has few all-round drivers. There are, however, some remarkably fine men, and a veteran amongst them is Barney Oldfield, who won his first car race in 1902, when he was twenty-three years old; that victory was secured with a car built by Henry Ford. Oldfield was born on a farm in Ohio, and sold newspapers to buy his first bicycle. He worked as bellboy in an hotel, then became a bicycle salesman—riding racing cycles at the same time—before he joined Henry Ford as a mechanic, afterwards to drive cars in early American events.

Oldfield's best work was done during the first years of motor racing, when he was engaged both in record attempts and in dirt-track work. His first race was on a dirt track, and it is from such events that almost all America's drivers have graduated—notably the late Frank Lockhart. When Frank Lockhart was killed in attempting the land-speed record with his 'Black Hawk' Stutz, in 1928, America lost one of her cleverest drivers. He was barely twenty-four years of age, and prepared his own cars, for he had great engineering knowledge; he achieved a speed of 164 m.p.h. with a 1,500 c.c. Miller on a dry lake in California, and won the Indianapolis race in 1926.

The depth of Lockhart's engineering ability may be judged from the fact that, in 1928, his 'Black Hawk' Stutz attained a speed in excess of 200 m.p.h., even though it was fitted with only a three-litre engine. In spite of the advances which have since been made in knowledge and technique, it is only within the last year that similar speeds have been reached with machines powered by engines so small as this. In actual fact, no car with a three-litre engine has matched Lockhart's speed, since the Mercédès and the Auto-Unions have approximately five-litre engines.

A man who may be regarded as one of America's finest drivers is Tommy Milton who, incidentally, has the handicap of possessing only one sound eye. He has twice won the Indianapolis race, and has held the national

125 JOHN COBB

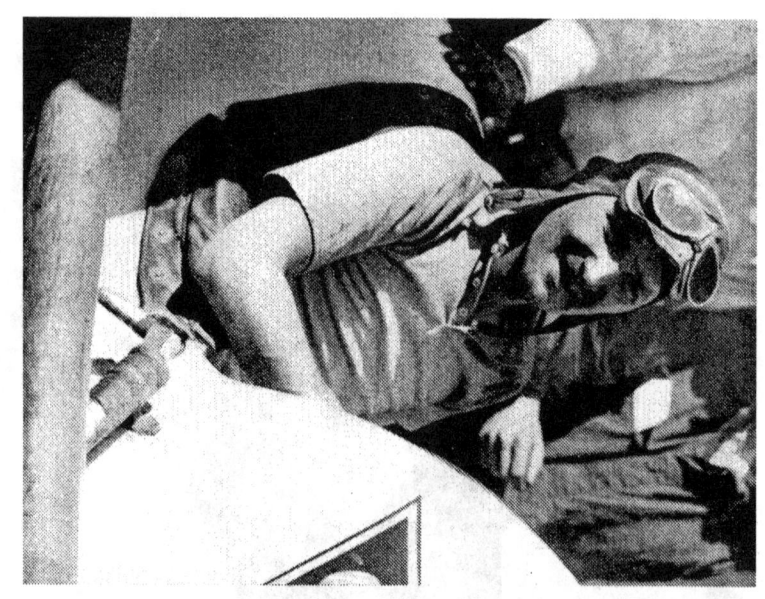

126 'WILD BILL' CUMMINGS

127 KELLY PETILLO

128 HON. BRIAN LEWIS

129 'TIM' ROSE-RICHARDS

130 A CHARACTERISTIC IMPRESSION OF THE LATE SIR HENRY BIRKIN, PHOTOGRAPHED WITH SIR MALCOLM CAMPBELL AT BROOKLANDS JUST BEFORE THE START OF A HANDICAP RACE

championship. Ranking with him in ability was Jimmy Murphy, who was killed in a smash on a one-mile dirt track at Syracuse in 1924, the year in which he held the championship. Prior to his fatal smash, he won three races in three months on board tracks, each event counting towards the championship, while in 1921 he had won the French Grand Prix.

The American champion for 1934 was William Cummings, of Indianapolis, whose reputation as one of the most dashing drivers in the U.S.A. has earned him the nickname of 'Wild Bill.' Aged twenty-eight, he had been driving for more than five years when he secured the championship, and in 1930 he set up a world's dirt-track record for a one hundred miles event at Syracuse, averaging 83·48 m.p.h. Throughout his career his racing luck had never been good, but this changed for the Indianapolis race of 1934, when he won at the record speed of 104·86 m.p.h.

These American drivers all raced on dirt or board tracks, and only Frank Lockhart attempted serious record work; the records which Oldfield established in the early years were splendid efforts, but were normally over very short distances.

Only in 1934 did America seriously enter into the field for records, when D. A. ('Ab') Jenkins registered amazing speeds over the Bonneville salt flats near Salt Lake City, Utah. He averaged 127·22 m.p.h. for twenty-four hours, and covered his first thousand miles at over 130 m.p.h. It is interesting to notice that Jenkins came into prominence only as a result of these records, and that he is not actively engaged in track work.

As well known in America as in England is Sir Malcolm Campbell, whose first experience in competitive sport was in a motor-cycle trial in 1906, and who afterwards became famous both as a racing driver and as a world's record breaker. He was the first man officially to raise the world's land-speed record to 150 m.p.h.—this was in 1925. He was the first to achieve four miles a minute, and went on to reach 250 m.p.h., then to pass 275 m.p.h. and his efforts to lift the speed to 300 m.p.h. were eventually successful in September 1935.

Although his career has involved experience in every class of high-speed event, and a great deal of hill climbing, his world-wide fame comes mainly from record breaking. His energy is very great, and the popularity that he has gained through his splendid achievements is fully deserved by a fine personality. All his record-breaking attempts have been financed by himself, although their cost has, at times, been very great. He was fifty years of age on March 11th, 1935, and his very long and successful career makes him a veteran amongst racing drivers.

One of the very few Englishmen to have achieved any reputation on the Continent is Lord Howe, popular president of the British Racing Drivers' Club. His first race was at Brooklands in 1928, and his first real success was in 1931 when, partnered by the late Sir Henry Birkin, he drove an Alfa-Romeo to victory at Le Mans, averaging 78·31 m.p.h. for the twenty-four hours.

Since then he has competed in most of the important Grands Prix, but he has rarely been granted good racing luck, and after his first win at Le Mans he had to wait two years before, in 1933, he won the 1,500 c.c. class in the Eifel International race at the Nurburg Ring, driving a Delage. His driving is always very cool and skilful, and it is rarely that he finds himself in an untoward

131 F. W. ('FREDDIE') DIXON

132 CAPTAIN G. E. T. EYSTON WITH ALBERT DENLY, HIS CO-DRIVER AND MECHANIC

situation. Possibly his narrowest escape occurred at Monza, during 1932, and the fact that he was left unhurt is one of the miracles of motor racing.

His car skidded as he entered a bend at the tails of three other machines, his Delage sliding sideways off the track, leaping a ditch and striking a tree. The impact cut one front wheel clean off its axle, while the machine shot onward and struck another tree with such force that the frame of the car was bent around the trunk. The curvature was such that the end of the front axle was only a few inches away from the rear of the car, and the frame had to be cut in two before the machine could be removed.

When Lord Howe was extricated, those who had rushed to his assistance refused to believe that he was unhurt and forced him on to a stretcher; actually, he was quite uninjured, and presently walked back to his pit.

Although Lord Howe occasionally appears at Shelsley Walsh with success, and in long-distance Brooklands events, his obvious preference is for Continental road racing where, it is generally admitted, the worth of men and machines is best tested. But the conditions which govern racing in the British Isles do not offer our own drivers a reasonable opportunity of proving themselves.

Our only important road race is the Tourist Trophy, although Donington Park is providing some first-class events, and other private road courses may soon be available in England. Our only 'round-the-houses' race of any merit is that held in Douglas, Isle of Man. Our one good hill climb is at Shelsley Walsh, and our only track is Brooklands, which is not the best possible venue for record breaking, while the demands of modern high-speed cars reveal that the course has certain unavoidable deficiencies for extremely fast work.

MOTOR RACING AND RECORD BREAKING

In addition, we have no manufacturers producing Grand Prix type machines, because our motor industry is under special restrictions which do not obtain on the Continent. Our roads in England have never seen organized road racing, and it is lack of opportunity—and lack of machines—which prevent our own drivers striving for Grand Prix honours against men on the Continent. In spite of all this, however, our men have done great things at Le Mans, Montlhèry, and some of the principal road races abroad.

We have the Hon. Brian Lewis, 'Tim' Rose-Richards, C. Penn-Hughes, 'Freddie' Dixon—it is possible to name a dozen other drivers who, given the cars and the opportunity, could produce the form and the skill of Continental 'cracks.'

Now and again in the past one of our men has gained the chance to show what he could do—notably the late Sir Henry Birkin. He won fame at Le Mans, and would certainly have been a great force in present-day events in Europe had not a burn from an exhaust pipe in the Grand Prix of Tripoli set up the blood-poisoning from which he died. And there was J. G. Parry Thomas, a magnificent driver and a wonderful engineer, who crashed while attempting records at Pendine. The world of British motor racing lost much when these two passed on, but their memory serves as a spur to the rest.

It is in the example of such men as Segrave and Frank Lockhart, Louis Chiron and Oldfield, Nuvolari and Birkin, that the young driver who still awaits his chance may find hope. They began with little except their nerve and knowledge, but they found great fame.

That England can hold her own if ever her manufacturers turn to Grand Prix cars is proved by what has been done in other fields. Throughout the world no

PERSONALITIES

country has so fine a reputation for motor engineering, and we excel in the production of racing machines of under 1,500 c.c. It is in the proving of those machines that our own drivers have given great service and, in so doing, many of them have built up reputations for fine, sound driving, even though they may not have achieved world-wide fame.

Apropos of this, there is one thing worth remembering; it is not by victories that motor racing progresses, but by the failures which, when overcome, make further victories possible.

A man who drives and fails to win, but who improves his car and drives again, actually does more for motor racing than the driver who gains some great victory. The latter sets a mark for others to surpass; it is the men who struggle to beat what he has done who do most for racing cars, and for the normal machines which are eventually built upon their design.

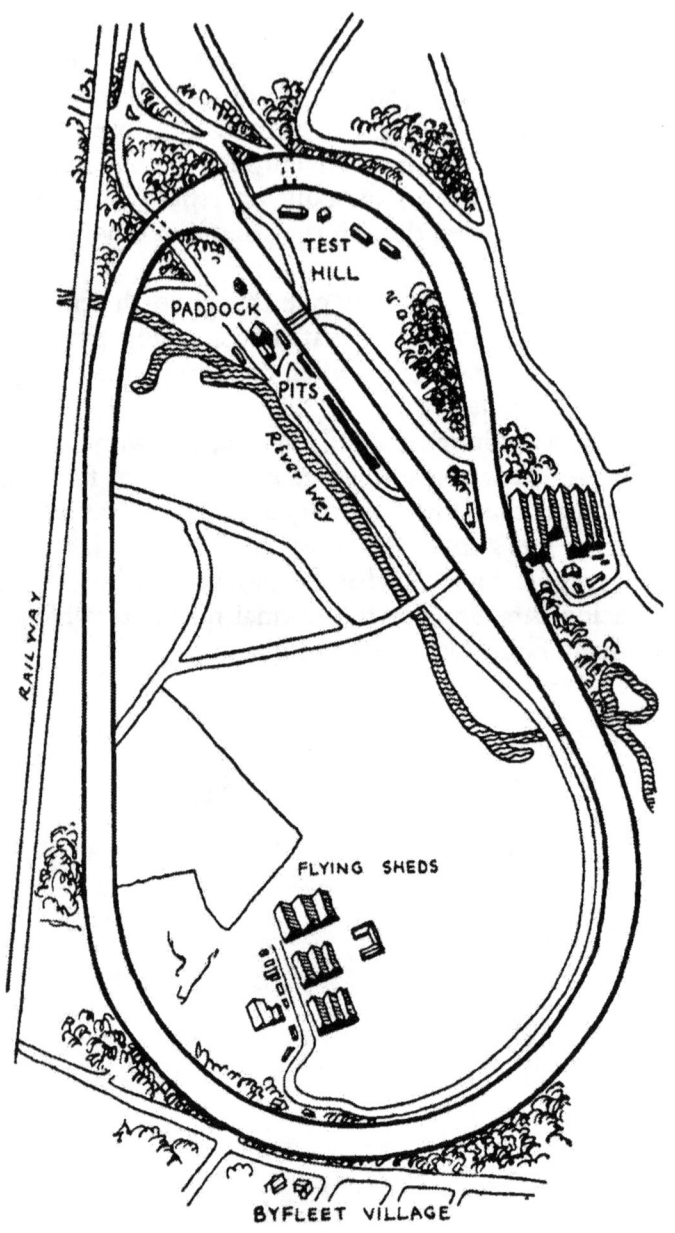

BROOKLANDS TRACK. THE LAP LENGTH IS 2 MILES, 1,350 YARDS

DIAGRAMS

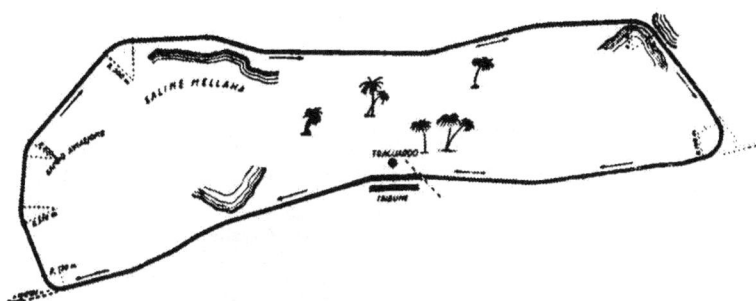

THE MELLAHA CIRCUIT, OVER WHICH THE GRAND PRIX OF TRIPOLI IS RUN. THE LAP DISTANCE IS 8·18 MILES

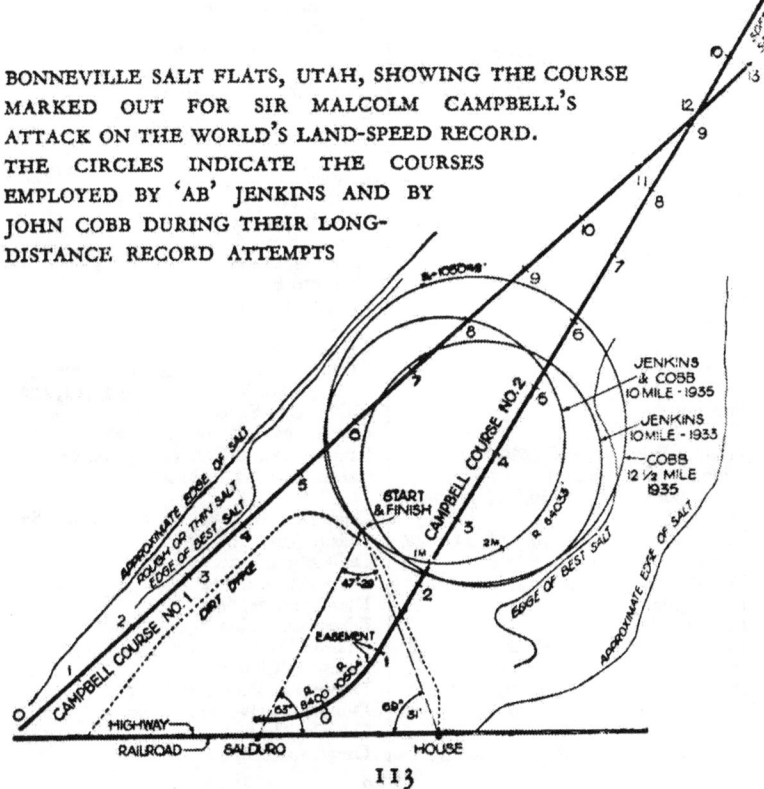

BONNEVILLE SALT FLATS, UTAH, SHOWING THE COURSE MARKED OUT FOR SIR MALCOLM CAMPBELL'S ATTACK ON THE WORLD'S LAND-SPEED RECORD. THE CIRCLES INDICATE THE COURSES EMPLOYED BY 'AB' JENKINS AND BY JOHN COBB DURING THEIR LONG-DISTANCE RECORD ATTEMPTS

INDEX TO TEXT AND ILLUSTRATIONS

(The numerals in italics denote the *figure numbers* of the illustrations)

Adler (car), *61*
Africa, *see* Algiers, Tripoli, Tunis
Alfa-Romeo (cars), 17, 18, 20, 64, 66, 76, 80, 93, 96, 97, 103, 104, 108; *14, 17, 42, 71, 86, 89, 94*
Algiers, Grand Prix, *18*
Altoona Speedway, 30, 71; *79*
American Automobile Association, 73
Ards Circuit, 17
Arnage, 80
Atlantic City, 70
Automobile Club of France, 4, 5
Auto-Union (cars), 32, 66, 76, 96, 104, 105, 106; *34, 49, 50, 53, 70*
Avus Grand Prix, 32
Avus Track, 31, 32, 37; *28, 49, 59, 61, 66, 103*

'Babs,' 90, 91
Barbieri, M., 94
Barcelona, *24*
Belgian Grand Prix, *13*
Belgian Grand Prix de Vingt-Quatre Heures, 81
Bennett, Gordon: races, 2, 4
Benoist, Robert, 67, 68
Bentley (cars), 77, 78, 81; *90*
Beverley Hills, 70
Bible, Lee, 56
Biella, 44; *43, 44*
Bignami, 83
Bignan (car), 77, 78
Birkin, Sir Henry, 108; *130*
'Blue Bird,' 60; *64, 65*
Board tracks, 30, 31, 69, 70, 71; *79*
Bol d'Or, *91*
Bonneville Salt-beds, 59, 107, 113; *72*
Bordino, Pietro, 89
Borzacchini, Umberto, 34, 94; *99*
Boyer, Joe, 71
Brescia-Rome, 82
British Racing Drivers' Club, 26, 108
Brivio, Antonio, 97
Brooklands track, 6, 26, 27, 36, 59, 82, 92, 109, 112; *11, 26, 29, 57, 88, 90, 101, 109*
Bugatti (cars), 67, 68, 102, 104; *39*

Caltavuturo, 85
Campari, Cavaliere Giuseppe, 34, 94
Campbell, Sir Malcolm, 57, 60, 61, 107, 108; *63, 65, 111, 130*
Campofelice, 86
Caracciola, Rudolf, 8, 66, 97, 104, 105; *10, 12, 16, 17, 66, 114*
Castelbarco, 94
Cattaneo, 67
Cerda, 85
Charlotte, North Carolina, 71
Château-Thierry, 67, 68
Chicago, 75
Chinetti, Louis, 80; *86*
Chiron, Louis, 11, 13, 21, 40, 81, 96, 102, 103, 104, 110; *112*
Circuito di Biella, 44; *43, 44*
Circuito Bordino, 18
Citroën (car), 59
Coatalen, Louis, 101
Cobb, John, 58, 59, 113; *125*
Colours, racing, 2
Comer, Fred, 71
Comminges, 20, 21
Comotti, Franco, 20
Coppa Acerbo, 100
Cotati, 70
Couard Bends, 15
Crashes, 3, 4, 30, 33, 34, 56, 67, 68, 71, 72, 78, 80, 89-94; *47, 94-99, 101, 102*
Culver City Speedway, 70; *32*
Cummings, Bill, 29, 107; *126*
Czaykowski, Count, 32, 33, 93, 94
Czechoslovakia, 105; *23*

Daytona Beach, 54, 60, 61; *63, 64, 67*
Delage (car), 108, 109
Della Stufa, 93
Denly, Albert, *132*
Diesel engine, 60
Dirt-track racing, 69; *80, 106*
Dixon, 'Freddie,' 110; *41, 56, 131*
Dodson, 'Charley,' 22
Donington Park circuit, 21
Double-Twelve, 82; *88, 90*
Douglas, Isle of Man, 41, 42, 109; *45*
Dreyfus, René, 40

INDEX TO TEXT AND ILLUSTRATIONS

Driving-chains, 90
Duesenberg (cars), 5, 73, 76, 93; *57*
Duff, J. F., 77, 78
Duray, Leon, 28

Eifel International race, 108
E.R.A. (car), 75
Escape road, 95
Etancelin, Philippe, 40; *86*
European Grand Prix, 33
Eyston, Captain G. E. T., 73, *132*

Fagioli, Luigi, 39; *38*, *118*
Ferrari *scuderia*, 20, 21, 104
Fiat (car), 5
First-aid on the race-track, 51; *103*
Ford (cars), 106
Forêt Corner, 16
Four-wheel drive, 68
Freiburg, 62
Fresno, 70

Gabriel, 4
German Grand Prix, 36
Giro d'Italia, 86
Grand Prix d'Algiers, *18*
Grand Prix de Comminges, 20, 21
Grand Prix de Czechoslovakia, *23*
Grand Prix d'Endurance, 77, 78; *84*, *94*
Grand Prix de la Marne, 10, 14; *13*, *14*
Grand Prix de Monaco, 38; *38*
Grand Prix de Nice, *40*
Grand Prix de Pau, *37*

Hartz, Harry, 70
Haugdahl, Sig., 54, 55
Hill climbing, 62 ff., 99
Hotchkiss (car), 62
Howe, Lord, 83, 108, 109; *39*, *89*, *124*

Indianapolis Speedway, 6, 28, 37, 76, 106; *30*, *31*, *102*, *108*
International Class records, 59

Jenkins, D. A., 107, 113

Kansas City, 71
Keech, Ray, 72
Klausen Pass, 65, 66

La Baule, *48*
Lagonda (car), *85*
Lakes, dry, as tracks, 8
La Marne, 10, 14; *13*, *14*
Lancia (car), 86

Langhorne dirt track, *81*
La Turbie hill, 102
Lautenschlager, 5; *4*
Legion Ascot Speedway, 95, *98*
Lehoux, 21
Le Mans, 6, 78, 80, 82, 84, 87, 108; *87*
Les Biscomes, 16
Levassor, Emile, 1
Lewis, Hon. Brian, *128*
Linas-Montlhèry autodrome, 7, 15, 25, 34, 37, 59, 92; *17*, *60*, *62*
Littorio track, 86
Lockhart, Frank, 56, 70, 106, 107, 110
Lurani, Count, *92*

Magic Midget (car), *58*
Mannin Beg race, 42; *41*, *45*
Maserati (cars), 64, 95; *39*, *46*, *76*
Materassi, Emilio, 33
Mays, Raymond, 65
Mellaha circuit, 113
Mercédès-Benz (cars), 39, 66, 67, 96, 97, 104, 105, 106; *4*, *10*, *12*, *15*, *17*, *66*
Meyer, Louis, 72
M.G. (cars), 17, 18, 42, 81, 103; *20*, *93*
Midget car championship, 75; *82*, *83*
Mille Miglia races, 6, 82, 84, 86, 87; *6*, *92*, *93*
Miller (car), 28, 70, 73, 106
Milton, Tommy, 106; *123*
Mines Field Aerodrome, 74, 75; *107*
Miramas, 7, 36
Modena, 44
Moll, Guy, 11, 12, 40, 93, 94, 96; *100*, *117*
Monaco, 7, 38, 45; *38*
Mont Ventoux, 62, 65; *76*, *78*
Montlhèry. *See* Linas-Montlhèry
Montreux, 46
Monza Speedway, 7, 33, 37, 109; *10*, *34*, *35*, *54*, *99*
Morgen, Otto von, 2
Mors (car), 4
Mulders Drift Hill, 77
Mulsanne Corner, 79, 80
Murphy, Jimmy, 3, 76, 107

Napier-Railton (cars), 35, 58; *11*
National Championships, 73
Nazarro, Biagio, 89
Nazarro, Felice, 88, 89
New York, 75
Nice, 42, 43; *40*
Nîmes, 44
Nurburg Ring, 7, 35, 36, 105, 108; *36*

Nuvolari, Tazio, 8, 11, 12, 14, 19, 40, 80, 96, 103, 104, 110; *113*

Oldfield, Barney, 105, 106, 107, 110; *120*
Opel Rocket (car), 101; *47*
'Outlaw' dirt-tracks, 73

Paris-Bordeaux-Paris, 1
Paris-Madrid, 2, 4, 82
Paris-Vienna, 2
Pau, Grand Prix de, 37
Pendine Sands, 90, 91
Penn-Hughes, C., 110
Penya Rhin Grand Prix, 24, *105*
Pescara Circuit, 13; *12*, *89*
Petillo, Kelly, 29, 74; *127*
Peugeot (cars), 76
Pike's Peak, 66
Pintacuda, 93
Pit-work, 46–53; *51*, *52*, *54*, *55*, *66*

Raticosa Pass, 83
Record breaking, 100
Reims, 10, 11
Resta, Dario, 92, 93
Riley (car), *41*
Rockingham Speedway, 30
Rolls-Bentley (car), 18
Rose-Richards, Tim, 110; *129*
Ruggieri, 92

St. Gaudens, 19
Salem, 71
San Carlos, 70
San Martin, 36
Sand, racing on, 8
Sarles, Rosco, 71
Sarthe circuit, 77
Segrave, Sir Henry, 56, 90, 91, 101, 102, 103, 110; *110*
Shelsley Walsh Hill, 62, 63, 64, 109; *75*

'Silver Bullet,' 67
Sitges, 36
'Speed of the Wind,' 73
Stelvio Pass, 64; *74*
Stewart, Mrs. Gwenda, *121*
Straight, Whitney, 12, 20, 64, 65; *46*, *57*, *76*, *119*
Strasburg, 88
Stuck, Hans von, 32, 66, 96, 105; *19*, *59*, *68*, *69*, *116*
Sunbeam (car), 90, 91
Swiss Grand Prix, 105
Syracuse, 107

Tacoma, 71
Tadini, Mario, 64
Targa Abruzzo, *89*
Targa Florio, 85, 86
Taruffi, Piero, 95, 96
Thillois turn, 11
Thomas, J. G. Parry, 90, 91, 110; *122*
Tourist Trophy races, 17, 18, 103, 109; *22*
Track racing, 99
'Triplex' (car), 56
Tripoli Grand Prix, 8, 95, 97, 113; *7*, *15*
Trossi, Count, 21, 93; *42*, *43*

Uniontown, Pennsylvania, 71

Vanes, special, 65
Varzi, Achille, 11, 12, 21, 31, 40, 43, 83, 96, 103, 104; *17*, *44*, *55*, *115*
Versailles, 1, 2
Vichy, Grand Prix de, *42*

Wheels, balance of, 55
Wilcox, Howard, 71
Wind-brakes, 65
Woodbridge dirt-track, N.J., 96, *104*

Zborowski, Count Louis, 90

www.ingramcontent.com/pod-product-compliance
Lightning Source LLC
Chambersburg PA
CBHW070645160426
43194CB00009B/1592